T0248247

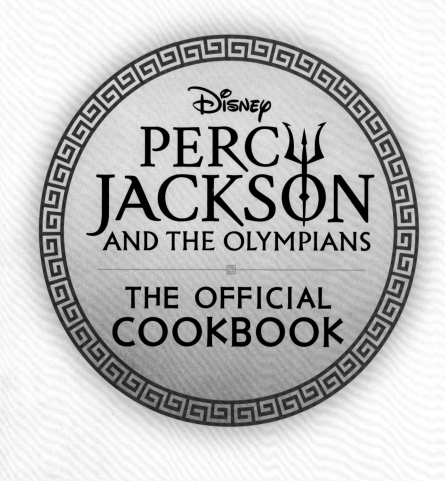

Disney

PERCY JACKSON
AND THE OLYMPIANS

THE OFFICIAL
COOKBOOK

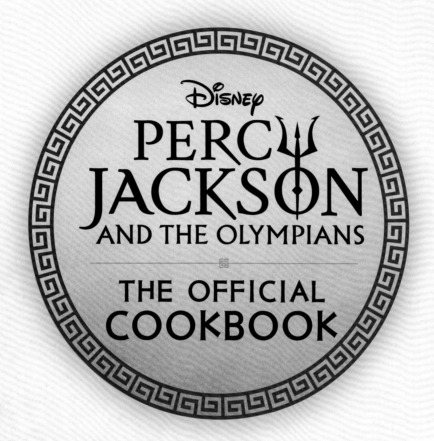

Disney

PERCY JACKSON

AND THE OLYMPIANS

THE OFFICIAL COOKBOOK

by Jarrett Melendez

INSIGHT
EDITIONS

SAN RAFAEL · LOS ANGELES · LONDON

CONTENTS

INTRODUCTION

Hello, heroes and heroes-in-the-making!

   If you know anything about me, you know that I love eating. My very favorite things to consume are aluminum cans and bean-and-cheese enchiladas. But a satyr, especially an aspiring Searcher, cannot live on cans and enchiladas alone. Believe me, I've tried, and it wasn't pretty.

   Food is important—it's how we stay alive, but it's also how we connect with other people. We've got it pretty easy at Camp Half-Blood, with the dryads preparing all our meals for us. But when you're on the go, like I've been with Percy Jackson and Annabeth Chase, you might find yourself in need of fuel when there's not a single wood nymph in sight. Our first quest took us from Camp Half-Blood to New York to St. Louis to Los Angeles and . . . oof . . . the Underworld. No disrespect to Hades, of course! He's done some really interesting things with the place. Very, um, homey.

   Anyway, I picked up a TON of recipes on that journey and decided it would be fun to collect them in a book so we can revisit our favorites whenever we want (without a side of world-ending peril). There are regional specialties from different locations, e.g., New York-style bagels and pizza; breads, BBQ, and s'mores like the dryads make for us at camp; gooey butter cake from St. Louis; and tons of classic diner fare like burgers, fries, and milkshakes. Some dishes are inspired by places we visited or the Kindly Ones we encountered along the way and, of course, there are lots of traditional Greek dishes. We've even got some Sally Jackson originals, like her famous seven-layer dip, and Percy's favorite blue chocolate chip cookies. Naturally, I had Annabeth review everything. She added a few tips and clever suggestions where she saw fit. ⟵——————— somebody had to do it. —Annabeth

   Don't worry—I would never make a collection of beloved recipes without including one for bean-and-cheese enchiladas. After just one bite, you'll know why I'm so obsessed with them. My hope for this book, apart from convincing you to join my enchilada fan club, is that you'll find some new favorite dishes in it as you go on your own cooking journey. Think of it this way: you get to reap the benefits of one of the most harrowing quests of my short little satyr life without all the danger and, y'know, minor despair. Lucky you!

                                                                    —Grover Underwood

CHAPTER ONE

BREADS: THE RISE OF A HERO

Like dough before it can be baked, a hero must rise. And once risen, that hero is probably going to be put through some trials by fire (very literally, in some cases . . . ouch). In this chapter, you'll find a collection of recipes for different breads that Percy, Annabeth, and I enjoyed from different locations our quest took us. Think bagels from Manhattan, and an array of classic Greek breads, like those the dryads prepare at Camp Half-Blood or that you might find if you ever take that elevator up to Mt. Olympus.

NEW YORK-STYLE BAGELS

YIELD: 12 BAGELS ▪ TIME: 3 HOURS ▪ V

You don't have to walk too far from, well, anywhere to find a bagel shop in New York City. Even if you're already standing in front of one, you're probably just a drachma's throw away from the next. Most of them tout themselves as having the best bagels in New York. And trust me, I've seen some heated and colorful discussions among New Yorkers about which shop actually DOES have the best bagels. As for me, I say whichever bagel YOU think is best IS the best—for you! We picked up this recipe in Manhattan, and even though they say a bagel made anywhere outside the city isn't quite the same—something about the water, I guess—this produces very tasty ones. They've even been known to cure Percy's homesickness . . . for a little while, anyway.

BAGEL DOUGH:	BOILING SOLUTION:	EGG WASH AND TOPPINGS:
1⅔ cups lukewarm water	½ gallon water	1 egg white
1 tablespoon barley malt syrup	1 tablespoon barley malt syrup	1 tablespoon water
2 teaspoons active dry yeast	1 teaspoon baking soda	Sesame seeds, poppy seeds, or Everything Bagel seasoning
5 cups bread flour		
1 tablespoon kosher salt		

1. **TO MAKE THE BAGEL DOUGH:** In a small bowl, stir together the lukewarm water and the barley malt syrup until the syrup dissolves. Stir in the yeast and let the mixture sit for 5 to 10 minutes, until foamy.

2. Whisk together the flour and salt in a large bowl either by hand or using a stand mixer fitted with the dough hook attachment. Set the mixer on low and add the yeast mixture. Let mix until a shaggy dough forms, 3 to 5 minutes. Increase whisking speed to medium and continue kneading until the dough is smooth and elastic, 10 to 15 minutes longer.

3. Lightly oil a large bowl, transfer the dough to it, and cover tightly with a lid or plastic wrap. Let the dough sit until well puffed and not quite doubled in volume, about 60 to 90 minutes. At this point, you can transfer the dough to the fridge and let it ferment for up to 5 days for extra-flavorful bagels. If you do this, let the dough sit out for 2 hours to come to room temperature before proceeding to the next step.

4. Line two half-sheet pans with sheets of parchment. Divide the dough into 12 equal portions. Pre-shape each portion into a ball by pulling the top of the dough down to the bottom. To even out the edges, place your first dough ball, smooth-side up, on a clean work surface. Cup it with your one hand so that your fingers are just barely touching the sides of the dough and your fingertips are resting on your work surface. Rotate your fingertips along this surface in a clockwise motion until the top of the dough is pulled tight and smooth. Repeat for each dough ball, then transfer all twelve to the prepared pans—six per pan. Lightly cover with plastic wrap and let rest until puffed slightly, 30 to 45 minutes.

5. Place racks on the upper and lower third positions of the oven, then preheat to 425°F.

6. **TO MAKE THE BOILING SOLUTION:** Bring the water, barley malt syrup, and baking soda to a boil in a large pot over medium-high heat.

7. **TO MAKE THE EGG WASH AND PREPARE THE TOPPINGS:** Whisk the egg white and water together in a small bowl. Pour your preferred toppings into a separate wide, shallow bowl.

8. Poke a hole with your index finger into one of the waiting dough balls until you break through the dough and form a small hole. Gently stretch the dough out until the hole is about 1½ to 2 inches wide and the bagel is about 4 or 5 inches across. Repeat with the remaining dough balls.

9. Boil the bagels for 30 seconds on each side before transferring them to a wire rack to drain. It can help to boil just three at a time. Once all the bagels are on the rack, brush them all over with the egg wash and then dip both sides in your preferred toppings before transferring the bagels back to the prepared pans.

10. Bake the bagels for 15 to 20 minutes, rotating the pans halfway through, until they are golden brown and register 190°F on an instant-read thermometer inserted into the thickest part of the bagel. Let cool on wire racks before storing at room temperature in airtight containers for up to 3 days.

KOULOURIA

YIELD: 12 KOULOURIA ▪ TIME: 2 HOURS 30 MINUTES ▪ V

Grover, it may be worth mentioning that both the ingredients and cooking process make these quite different from bagels! Still delicious, with a unique taste and texture. —Annabeth

The first time the dryads served me one of these bread rings at Camp Half-Blood, I was blown away. Koulouria have been a staple street food in Greece for centuries, and I can see why. Their crispy outside, crunchy sesame seeds, and chewy center make them irresistible, especially when still warm from the oven. I once asked a dryad how many koulouria they'd baked over the years. The tree nymph stared into the distance while they did the math and then quickly walked away without answering. I spent the rest of the week avoiding Mr. D just in case he felt I'd caused offense to the nature spirit. But koulouria keep showing up at mealtimes, so it can't have been that big a deal . . . right? We usually have these with breakfast, but they're great any time of day, with a meal or by themselves as a quick snack.

KOULOURIA DOUGH:
1 cup lukewarm water
2 tablespoons honey
2 teaspoons active dry yeast
2½ cups all-purpose flour
½ cup whole wheat flour
1 teaspoon kosher salt

COATING:
2 cups water, room temperature
¼ cup honey
2 cups toasted sesame seeds

1. **TO MAKE THE DOUGH:** In a small bowl, stir the water and honey together until the honey dissolves. Stir in the yeast and let the mixture sit for 5 to 10 minutes, until foamy.

2. In a large mixing bowl or the bowl of a stand mixer, whisk together the all-purpose and whole wheat flours, along with salt, either by hand or using the mixer's dough hook attachment. Set the mixer on low and add the yeast mixture. Mix for 1 minute to hydrate the flour, then increase the speed to medium. Mix until a soft dough forms, 8 to 10 minutes.

3. Transfer the dough to a lightly greased large bowl, cover, and let proof until the dough doubles in volume, 60 to 90 minutes.

4. Toward the end of the rising time, place two oven racks at the lower and upper third positions in the oven and preheat to 400°F. Line two half-sheet pans with parchment paper.

5. **TO PREPARE THE COATING:** Whisk the water and honey together in a wide bowl. Place the sesame seeds in a separate wide, shallow bowl.

6. **TO MAKE THE KOULOURIA:** Divide the dough into 12 equal portions. Roll 1 portion of dough into a 12-inch-long log, allowing the ends to taper slightly. Join the ends together to make a ring and place this on a clean work surface. Roll the ends together with the palm of your hand to seal the ring. Repeat the shaping process with the remaining 11 portions of dough.

7. Dip 1 dough ring into the water-and-honey mixture, shake off the excess moisture, then dip both sides of the ring in the sesame seeds. Transfer the coated ring to one of the prepared sheet pans, then repeat the process until you have six coated rings per pan.

8. Bake the rings for 18 to 20 minutes, until deep golden brown and firm, rotating the pans about halfway through the baking time. Let the koulouria cool slightly on the pans for 5 minutes, then transfer them to a wire rack to cool completely.

LADENIA

YIELD: ONE 9-BY-13-INCH LADENIA ▪ TIME: 3 HOURS 30 MINUTES ▪ V

You might hear some folks call this "Greek pizza," because it's bread with tomato. Some versions of ladenia do look like a traditional pizza—round, with a thin crust. Other recipes call for a thicker bread that's baked in a rectangular baking pan, like the Italian focaccia, which this recipe resembles. Come to think of it, I guess I've seen deep-dish pizzas that look like ladenia in my travels, too. Look, I don't want anybody getting sidetracked by debate about what truly defines PIZZA. Annabeth and Percy do just fine arguing that one among themselves. Why don't we just say that it's Greek, and its own thing, and can be prepared in lots of ways, and hope that everyone is happy and gets along. Cool? Cool. Speaking of cool, what's cool about this bread is that it's great either warm or at room temperature, making it a wise and logical choice to pack for an outing . . . or a perilous quest. At least, that's what Annabeth likes to remind me. You can also use any type of tomato you prefer. But for the best tasting ladenia, I like using super flavorful heirloom tomatoes at the peak of their season in summertime.

3 cups bread flour	¼ cup olive oil, plus more for pan and drizzling	1½ teaspoon capers, drained and rinsed
2 teaspoons kosher salt	2 heirloom tomatoes, thinly sliced	1 teaspoon kosher salt
2 teaspoons instant yeast	¼ red onion, thinly sliced	Flake sea salt to taste
1¼ cups warm water		
2 teaspoons honey		

1. In a medium-size bowl or the bowl of a stand mixer, whisk together the flour and salt in a either by hand or using the mixer's dough hook attachment. Mix at low speed, adding the yeast, water, honey, and ¼ cup of olive oil. Continue mixing until a shaggy dough forms, then increase the speed to medium. Mix for 5 to 10 minutes, until the dough is smooth, elastic, and slightly sticky. If mixing by hand, knead for 15 to 20 minutes.

2. Transfer the dough to a large, well-oiled bowl and cover. Let the dough rise for 60 to 90 minutes, until well puffed and doubled in volume. Drizzle about 2 tablespoons of olive oil into a 9-by-13-inch baking dish. Tip the dough into the dish and gently stretch the dough out to fill the pan. Cover with a clean kitchen towel and let rest until puffed, 20 to 30 minutes.

3. Preheat the oven to 425°F. While the oven heats, prepare the toppings: In a colander, toss the tomatoes, onion, and capers together with the salt. Set the colander over a large bowl and let the toppings drain for 10 to 15 minutes.

4. Spread the tomatoes, onion, and capers over the top of the dough, drizzle with additional olive oil, then bake for 40 to 45 minutes, until golden brown. An instant-read thermometer should register 190°F when inserted into the center of the bread.

5. Sprinkle the bread with flake sea salt to taste. Allow ladenia to cool before cutting and serving.

ATHENIAN LOAF
(ELIOPSOMO)

YIELD: 1 LOAF ▪ TIME: 4 HOURS ▪ V

This loaf of bread does double-duty honoring the goddesses Demeter (goddess of grains and agriculture, for those not in the know) and Athena, who is NOT the goddess of olives (do not even make that joke around Annabeth) but does have a very strong association with them. You might call eliopsomo something of an overachiever or, as Percy might put it, "the Annabeth of breads." Whatever you call it, just know that it's delicious with its pockets of salty, briny olives, and bright aromatic herbs throughout. It's tasty and hearty enough to make a light meal on its own, but you could use slices of it to make sandwiches, or to have as a side with a larger meal. It's great toasted and spread with a little bit of honey—the sweetness goes nicely with the salty olives.

1¼ cups lukewarm water

1½ tablespoons honey

2½ teaspoons active dry yeast

3½ cups all-purpose flour

1 teaspoon kosher salt

1 teaspoon dried oregano

½ teaspoon dried rosemary

3 tablespoons olive oil

1 cup kalamata olives, drained and coarsely chopped, divided

1. Whisk the water, honey, and yeast together in a small bowl until dissolved. Let the mixture sit for 5 to 10 minutes, or until foamy.

2. In a medium-size bowl or the bowl of a stand mixer, whisk together the flour, salt, oregano, and rosemary either by hand or using the mixer's dough hook attachment. Mix at low speed, add the yeast mixture, and continue to mix until a shaggy dough forms, then add the olive oil. Increase the speed to medium and continue mixing until the dough is smooth (minus the teeny bits of dried herbs), 7 to 10 minutes. If mixing by hand, knead for 10 to 15 minutes, until smooth.

3. Transfer the dough to a large, oiled bowl. Cover the bowl and let the dough proof until it doubles in volume, 60 to 90 minutes.

4. Tip the dough out onto a clean work surface and divide into 4 roughly equal pieces. Flatten each piece into a round disc about ½ inch thick. Spread ⅓ of the olives over one dough round. Stack a second dough round over the olives and layer another ⅓ of the olives on top of that. Repeat the stacking and spread the remaining olives with the third dough round. Set the final disc of dough at the top, stretching and pulling until it fully envelops the previous layers of dough and olives. Cup your hands around the loaf and spin it clockwise, gently pulling down as you rotate the dough until the top is taut and smooth and the loaf is round.

5. Transfer the loaf to a sheet of parchment paper, then cover it with a clean kitchen towel. Let the dough rise until well puffed, 45 to 60 minutes. While the dough rises, place a large Dutch oven, lid and all, in the oven, then heat the oven to 500°F.

6. Remove the kitchen towel and deeply slash the dough 3 or 4 times across the top with a bread lame or very sharp knife. Open the oven and remove the lid of the Dutch oven. Using the corners of the sheet of parchment, lift the dough up and lower it into the hot Dutch oven, and then replace the lid. Close the oven door and lower the temperature to 450°F. Bake for 20 minutes, then remove the Dutch oven lid and bake for 10 to 15 minutes longer, until the loaf is a deep golden brown and an instant-read thermometer registers 190°F when inserted into the center of the bread.

7. Immediately transfer the bread from the Dutch oven to a wire cooling rack and let it cool to room temperature before slicing and eating. Keep leftover bread tightly wrapped at room temperature for up to 3 days.

GREEK VILLAGE BREAD

YIELD: 1 LOAF • TIME: 4 HOURS • V

Is there anything more comforting than a big hunk of warm, toasty bread? I mean for you non-aluminum-can-eating folks, that is. This bread is a mainstay at Camp Half-Blood because the dryads can start on it in the morning or even the day before and finish it in time to be served warm with dinner. Just about every meal comes with baskets of bread, and every basket holds a few loaves of this classic Greek staple. It's simple and mildly flavored, with a hint of sweetness and nuttiness, which make it a great side. It's especially popular on soup or stew nights, when you'll see campers toss their spoons aside and use this bread to mop up the last few bits of broth before sighing contentedly. Sometimes it's the little things that bring relief and joy in between training sessions, and this crusty loaf is definitely one of those little things.

1½ cups lukewarm water	2½ teaspoons active dry yeast	1½ teaspoons kosher salt
¼ cup lukewarm milk	3 cups bread flour	
2 tablespoons honey	1 cup semolina flour	

1. Whisk together the water, milk, honey, and yeast in a small bowl until the honey and yeast are dissolved. Let the mixture sit for 5 to 10 minutes, until foamy.

2. In a separate medium-size bowl or using the bowl of a stand mixer, whisk together the bread flour, semolina flour, and salt either by hand or using the mixer's dough hook attachment. Mix at low speed, then add the yeast mixture. Continue to mix until a shaggy dough forms. Increase the speed to medium and continue mixing until the dough is smooth and elastic, about 7 to 10 minutes longer. If mixing by hand, knead the dough for 10 to 20 minutes until it is smooth and elastic.

3. Transfer the dough to a lightly oiled bowl and cover. Let the dough proof until it doubles in volume, 60 to 90 minutes.

4. Tip the dough out onto a clean work surface. Cup your hands around the loaf and spin clockwise, gently pulling down as you rotate the dough until the top is taut and smooth and the loaf is round.

5. Transfer the loaf to a sheet of parchment paper, then cover with a clean kitchen towel. Let the dough rise until well puffed, 45 to 60 minutes. While the dough rises, place a large Dutch oven, lid and all, in the oven, then heat oven to 500°F.

6. Remove the kitchen towel and deeply slash the dough 3 or 4 times across the top with a bread lame or very sharp knife. Open the oven and remove the lid of the Dutch oven. Using the corners of the sheet of parchment, lift the dough up and lower it into the hot Dutch oven, then replace the lid. Close the oven door and lower the temperature to 450°F. Bake for 20 minutes, then remove the Dutch oven lid and bake for 15 to 20 minutes longer until the loaf is a deep golden brown and an instant-read thermometer registers 190°F when inserted into the center of the bread.

DAKTYLA

YIELD: MAKES 10 ROLLS ▪ TIME: 4 HOURS ▪ V

Greek language lesson time! (Don't groan—it's nice to learn new things.) So DAKTYLA means FINGERS in Greek. These rolls are long and thin, sort of like fingers, hence the name. Now here's a history lesson (okay, I admit, I got this move from Mr. Brunner; it was funny when he tried it on Percy): Way, wayyyy back, there were folks called the Daktyloi who were close to Zeus's mother, Rhea. And when Zeus was just a little baby, his father, Kronos, well, let's say he had his own approach to "family dinner." Zeus's mother hid the baby god of thunder in a cave and appointed the Daktyloi to protect him and keep him hidden from Kronos. It's possible these rustic little rolls get their name from those very god-protectors, and if there were actual campers in Cabin 1, I bet this would be their favorite bread.

3 cups bread flour, divided

½ cup fine cornmeal

1½ cups water

1½ teaspoons instant yeast

1½ teaspoons kosher salt

¼ cup toasted sesame seeds, plus more for sprinkling

2 teaspoons nigella seeds, plus more for sprinkling

2 tablespoons olive oil

1 large egg white

1 tablespoon water

1. Place 1 cup of the bread flour and all the cornmeal in a medium bowl or the bowl of a stand mixer. Whisk to combine, then stir in the water and yeast until smooth. Cover the bowl with plastic wrap and let the mixture sit for 1 hour.

2. Remove the plastic wrap and add the remaining 2 cups of flour and the salt, sesame seeds, nigella seeds, and olive oil to the bowl. Fit the dough hook attachment to the mixer and mix the dough until smooth and elastic, 7 to 10 minutes. If you don't have a stand mixer, you can make this dough by hand—knead for 15 to 20 minutes. Transfer the dough to a lightly oiled bowl and cover it with plastic wrap. Let the dough proof until it doubles in size, 60 to 90 minutes.

3. Line a half-sheet pan with parchment paper. Divide the dough into 10 equal pieces. Roll each piece of dough into a log about 1½ inches wide and about 4 inches long. Transfer the dough logs to the prepared pan, starting at one of the short sides and lining the logs up with about 1 inch of space between them. Cover the pan with lightly greased plastic wrap and let the logs rise until they're just touching, 45 to 60 minutes.

4. Preheat the oven to 375°F. Whisk together the egg white and 1 tablespoon water. Once the dough is ready to bake, brush the rolls with the egg wash and sprinkle them with sesame seeds and nigella seeds.

5. Bake the daktyla for 25 to 30 minutes, until they are golden and an instant-read thermometer registers 190°F when inserted in the center of the rolls. Serve warm or at room temperature.

CHAPTER TWO

BREAKFAST: THE QUEST BEGINS

The most important step to any quest is, well, the first one. After all, you can't start your quest without taking the first step, right? I feel the same way about breakfast: you can't start your day without a nice, filling meal. Now how you define that is up to you. That's why I've tried to include all kinds of recipes to start your day (or quest) with. In this chapter, you'll find everything from NYC staples like the classic BEC, to regional omelets Percy, Annabeth, and I discovered along our cross-country trip, to breakfast dishes inspired by the (eek) Underworld! Whichever dish you choose as the start of your day, it'll give you the energy you need to take that crucial first step.

BEC ON A BULKIE

YIELD: 4 SANDWICHES ▪ TIME: 40 MINUTES

New York City is absolutely riddled with delis, bodegas, and food carts that'll sell you a "BEC" on some kind of bread, whether it's a bagel or English muffin or a bulkie roll. A "bulkie," I know, is a New England-style sandwich roll, a bit like a hamburger bun. But larger and flakier. And "BEC," Percy tells me, is short for "bacon, egg, and cheese." I've heard that if you walk by certain high-volume spots in the city late at night (or very early in the morning, depending on your perspective), the smell of cooking grease fills the air as vendors begin making their BECs. It took me an embarrassingly long amount of time to realize that "saltpepperketchup" was actually three separate words and not some kind of local greeting. It's how a lot of folks customize their sandwich. This recipe makes four sandwiches, but you can scale it up or down to feed just one or two people or a whole camp of demigods.

---

8 slices thick-cut bacon

4 tablespoons salted butter, softened

4 bulkie rolls, split

6 large eggs

Kosher salt

Nonstick cooking spray

4 slices American cheese

Freshly ground black pepper

Ketchup

---

1. Heat the oven to 450°F. Set an oven-safe wire rack in a half-sheet pan. Lay the bacon on top of the wire rack and cook for 12 to 20 minutes, until it is deeply golden brown and crisp. Start checking at the 12-minute mark and remove the bacon when it reaches your preferred doneness.

2. Preheat a griddle over medium heat. Spread the butter on the cut sides of the bulkie rolls. Place the bulkie rolls, buttered-sides down, on the griddle and cook until golden brown, 3 to 5 minutes. Set the toasted rolls aside.

3. While the rolls toast, beat the eggs until slightly foamy and uniform in color. Beat in a large pinch of salt.

4. Spray the griddle with cooking spray, then pour the beaten eggs over the griddle in one large, thin layer. The egg should cook quite quickly. Once the top is just barely set, use a spatula to roll the sheet of cooked eggs up into a long rectangle.

5. Cut the egg rectangle into 4 equal-size squares. Top each square with a slice of American cheese. Transfer each square of egg and cheese to the bottom half of a roll. Top each with 2 slices of bacon, and season with additional salt, pepper, and ketchup as desired. Place the top halves of the rolls on the BECs and serve hot.

BLUEBERRY BUCKLE

YIELD: ONE 9-BY-13-INCH BUCKLE • TIME: 1 HOUR • V

Two things I know about Percy: he's got a bit of sweet tooth and he loves blue foods. I mean, there are plenty of other things I know about Percy, being his guardian and all. But those two details got me pretty far in the beginning. This particular recipe can be served for breakfast OR dessert. The blueberries don't technically look blue after you cook them and I haven't technically asked Sally Jackson if she would include it in her pantheon of blue food. But I personally think the taste makes it worthwhile either way. I highly recommend this recipe for any demigod looking for something pleasantly sweet to snack on as they greet the day.

STREUSEL TOPPING:
½ cup brown sugar
⅓ cup all-purpose flour
⅓ cup cold butter, cut into 1-inch pieces
½ teaspoon cinnamon
¼ teaspoon kosher salt
1 pinch nutmeg

BUCKLE:
½ cup butter, room temperature
1 cup granulated sugar
2 eggs, room temperature
1 teaspoon lemon zest
2 teaspoons vanilla
2¼ cups all-purpose flour
1 teaspoon baking powder
½ teaspoon baking soda
½ teaspoon kosher salt
½ teaspoon ground coriander
1 cup sour cream or Greek yogurt
2 cups blueberries

1. Grease a 9-by-13-inch baking dish. Preheat the oven to 350˚F.

2. **TO MAKE THE STREUSEL TOPPING:** Add all of the streusel topping ingredients to the bowl of a food processor. Pulse until the ingredients are well blended and take on a sandy texture. Set aside.

3. **TO MAKE THE BUCKLE:** Cream together the butter and sugar in a large bowl until light and fluffy, about 5 to 7 minutes. Mix in the eggs, one at a time, beating until thick and creamy. Mix in the lemon zest and vanilla until well incorporated.

4. Sift the flour, baking powder, baking soda, salt, and coriander together in a medium bowl. Add ⅓ the flour mixture to the butter mixture, then mix on low until just combined. Add half the sour cream and mix until just combined. Repeat, alternating between the flour and sour cream, making sure you end with the flour mixture.

5. Gently fold in the blueberries with a rubber spatula. Take this opportunity to scrape the bottom and sides of the bowl to ensure there are no pockets of dry flour. Pour the batter into the prepared dish—the batter will be quite thick and will need to be smoothed and leveled.

6. Sprinkle the streusel topping evenly over the batter. Bake the streusel-covered batter for 30 to 35 minutes, or until a cake tester inserted in the center of the buckle comes out clean. Allow to cool completely before serving.

BLUE SMOOTHIE

YIELD: 2 SMOOTHIES ▪ TIME: 5 MINUTES ▪ V, V+ (IF USING ALMOND MILK), GF

It's no secret that Percy is obsessed with blue foods and that Sally Jackson, saint that she is, goes to great lengths to make as many different blue dishes for her son as she can. Fortunately, she didn't have to go to much trouble to make up this blue smoothie. It comes together so quickly that it's a morning staple of the household. You'd think it might have blueberries in it, but they actually blend up to a sort of purple color. The blue color in this case doesn't come from dye, but from a type of algae called blue spirulina (maybe Annabeth should start calling Percy "Algae Brain" instead of "Seaweed Brain"). Honestly, it's a pretty fitting breakfast given his affinity with water . . .

1 cup frozen mango chunks

1 large banana, sliced

1 cup almond milk (or other milk)

¼ cup almond butter (or other nut butter)

2 teaspoons blue spirulina powder

¼ teaspoon ground cinnamon

¼ teaspoon vanilla extract

1. Add the ingredients to a blender in the order in which they're listed. Start the blender on low, and gradually increase the speed to high. Blend until smooth, 1 to 2 minutes.

2. Divide between two glasses and serve.

WHOLE-GRAIN BLUEBERRY PANCAKES
WITH STRAWBERRY-MAPLE SYRUP

YIELD: 4 SERVINGS ▪ TIME: 30 MINUTES ▪ V

We have to give major props to the campers in Demeter's and Mr. D's cabins for all the hard work they put into maintaining the strawberry fields and the Delphi Strawberry Service. The money earned from selling all those strawberries to local businesses helps keep Camp Half-Blood running. But even more important (okay, maybe not MORE important, but definitely AS important), we get to eat those luscious, juicy strawberries all year round. A camp breakfast favorite has to be these hearty whole-grain blueberry pancakes with strawberry-maple syrup. The sweet-tart berries mingling with warm ginger and earthy-sweet maple syrup is a combo that makes me excited to wake up in the morning. The best part is that you can make the syrup a couple days ahead of time so you're ready to top those fluffy, lightly spiced pancakes at a moment's notice. Although, if you ask Percy, he'd probably say the best part is that you can add blue food coloring. I guess that's how his mom would make them. Either way, they'll taste great!

STRAWBERRY-MAPLE SYRUP:

1 pound strawberries, hulled and quartered

⅓ cup maple syrup

½ teaspoon ground ginger

¼ teaspoon kosher salt

WHOLE-GRAIN PANCAKES:

2½ cups buttermilk, room temperature

3 large eggs, room temperature

2 tablespoons butter, melted and cooled slightly, plus more for griddle or pan

½ teaspoon electric blue gel food coloring

1 cup whole wheat flour

1 cup all-purpose flour

½ cup rolled oats

2 tablespoons granulated sugar

2 teaspoons baking powder

1 teaspoon ground cinnamon

¾ teaspoon kosher salt

½ teaspoon baking soda

½ cup blueberries

1. **TO MAKE THE SYRUP:** Combine the strawberries, maple syrup, ginger, and salt in a small saucepan over medium-low heat and cook, stirring occasionally, until the strawberries soften and release some of their juices, 7 to 10 minutes. Set aside to cool slightly. Syrup may be prepared up to 3 days in advance—keep it refrigerated in an airtight container until you're ready to use it.

2. **TO MAKE THE PANCAKES:** In a medium bowl, whisk the buttermilk and eggs together until smooth. Slowly pour in the butter, whisking constantly, until it is fully incorporated. Then stir in blue gel food coloring.

3. In a separate, large bowl, stir together the whole wheat flour, all-purpose flour, oats, sugar, baking powder, cinnamon, salt, and baking soda. Pour in the egg mixture and stir until it's just incorporated and no pockets of dry flour remain (it's okay if the batter has some lumps in it). Then gently fold in the blueberries.

4. Heat a large nonstick pan or griddle over medium heat. Add 1 tablespoon of unsalted butter, tilting the pan or griddle as the butter melts to coat the whole surface. Use a ⅓-cup measure to portion out pancakes onto the pan or griddle—if necessary, use the cup or the back of a spoon to spread the batter out a bit.

5. Cook each pancake until bubbles form and pop on its surface, about 2 minutes. Flip and cook for 2 minutes longer on the other side. If the pancakes are browning too quickly or not quickly enough, adjust the heat as needed. Repeat the cooking process until all of the batter has been used, using more butter if the pan is too dry and the pancakes start to stick a little. Serve with the strawberry-maple syrup.

GREEK YOGURT PARFAIT

YIELD: 1 PARFAIT, PLUS ABOUT 11 ADDITIONAL SERVINGS GRANOLA
TIME: 1 HOUR 20 MINUTES • V, GF

A yogurt parfait is such a delightful mix of textures to my satyr senses. The plump, juicy seasonal fruits (strawberries are always in season here at Camp Half-Blood, but use whatever you like!), the creamy yogurt, the sweet, sticky honey, and the satisfying crunch of granola—ooh, just thinking about it makes me want to clop-clop-clop my hooves in a happy dance. This recipe makes about three cups of granola, so there's extra for you to take on your quest. It's a great snack on its own, and it'll last you a whole week. That's particularly helpful when your hero's journey doesn't include access to a fridge. P.S. You really don't want to walk around with Greek yogurt in your pockets. I had to learn that the hard way.

GRANOLA:
1½ cups gluten-free rolled oats
½ cup pecans, coarsely chopped
½ cup coconut flakes
¼ cup pumpkin seeds
¼ cup sunflower seeds
⅓ cup maple syrup, warmed
1 tablespoon vanilla extract

1 tablespoon virgin coconut oil, melted and slightly cooled
1 large egg white (optional)
¾ teaspoon kosher salt
1 teaspoon ground cinnamon
¼ teaspoon ground ginger
¼ teaspoon ground cardamom

PARFAIT:
1 cup seasonal fruit
1 cup plain Greek yogurt
1 tablespoon honey
¼ cup granola

1. **TO MAKE THE GRANOLA:** Preheat the oven to 300°F. Line a half-sheet pan with parchment paper.

2. In a large bowl, toss the oats, pecans, coconut flakes, and pumpkin and sunflower seeds together. Set aside.

3. In a small bowl, whisk the maple syrup, vanilla extract, coconut oil, egg white, salt, cinnamon, ginger, and cardamom together until smooth.

4. Pour the maple syrup mixture over the oat mixture and stir until the ingredients are fully coated and well distributed. Pour the sweetened oat mixture into the prepared pan in a single, even layer. Bake for 45 to 60 minutes, stirring and tossing every 15 minutes, until the granola is crisp, golden, and dry throughout.

5. Transfer the pan to a wire cooling rack and let the granola cool to room temperature. Store granola in an airtight container at room temperature for up to 1 week.

6. **TO MAKE THE PARFAIT:** Slice or chop the fruit into bite-size pieces as needed and line the bottom of a wide bowl. Top the fruit with the yogurt. Drizzle the honey over the top of the yogurt, followed by the granola. Serve immediately.

LAVENDER LATTE

YIELD: 1 LATTE ▪ TIME: 20 MINUTES ▪ V, GF

I first saw these drinks being served in the Lotus Hotel and Casino—they had intricate little lotus-shaped designs in the foam. Percy explained that baristas call this LATTE ART and that, with practice, anybody can do it. I personally wouldn't know where to start, but I appreciate the creativity. There's something very satisfying about the aroma of these lavender lattes. You'd think the coffee would overpower the lavender, but the two scents mix and mingle in a way that's just irresistible. Lavender is very soothing and calming, and espresso puts pep in your footstep (or HOOFstep for us satyrs), so the drink SEEMS at odds with itself. Sounds like Lotus Eater trickery to me, but it smells so good, and everyone in the casino seemed to enjoy it. Maybe just one little sip . . .

LAVENDER SIMPLE SYRUP:
1 cup water
1 cup sugar
1 tablespoon dried lavender buds

LATTE:
1 teaspoon Lavender Simple Syrup (ingredients above)
2 shots espresso
1 cup hot milk

1. **TO MAKE THE LAVENDER SIMPLE SYRUP:** Combine the water, sugar, and lavender buds in a small pot over high heat and bring to a boil. Stir occasionally until the sugar dissolves.

2. Remove the pot from heat, cover, and let steep for 15 minutes. Strain out and discard the lavender buds, then let the syrup cool to room temperature. Keep refrigerated in an airtight container for up to 1 month.

3. **TO MAKE THE LATTE:** Pour 1 teaspoon of the prepared syrup into a mug. Pour the espresso over the syrup.

4. Use a steaming wand or milk frother to froth the milk. Pour the frothed milk over the espresso, pouring the foam in a pattern to create a design, if desired. Add more syrup to taste.

If using a steaming wand, start with cold milk.
—Annabeth

EGGS IN ASPHODEL

YIELD: 4 SERVINGS • TIME: 25 MINUTES • V, GF

The Fields of Asphodel is the part of the Underworld where most ordinary people end up after they've passed. It's sort of like a never-ending field in Kansas. I think Percy put it best when he said the souls there seem like they're waiting for a concert that's never going to start. It's neither good nor bad; it just is. This dish, on the other hand, is anything but neutral. It starts with a base of flavorful, spicy tomato sauce that's peppered with literal peppers for a touch of heat, pungent oregano, and briny olives. Then come the eggs, poached in the tomato sauce and topped with salty feta cheese. It's just spicy enough to make you sweat a little, like a quick foray into Hades's realm. Simply thinking about that place makes me sweat—no disrespect to Hades, of course!

2 tablespoons olive oil

1 small shallot, minced

4 garlic cloves, minced

½ teaspoon crushed Calabrian chile paste OR ¼ teaspoon crushed red pepper flakes

One 28-ounce can crushed tomatoes

1 teaspoon dried oregano

¼ cup kalamata olives, chopped

Kosher salt

8 large eggs

¼ cup feta cheese, crumbled and divided

1. Heat the oil in a large, high-walled sauté pan over medium-high heat. Add the shallot, garlic, and chile paste. Cook, stirring constantly, just until fragrant, about 1 minute.

2. Add the crushed tomatoes, oregano, and olives to the pan. Bring to a boil, stirring constantly, then reduce to a simmer. Cook, stirring occasionally, until sauce has reduced slightly, 5 to 7 minutes. Season to taste with kosher salt.

3. Crack an egg into a fine-mesh strainer set over a bowl, allowing the thin, watery part of the egg white go through the strainer. Gently tip the rest of the egg into the sauce. Repeat with the other eggs, discarding the watery portion of the egg whites when you're finished.

4. Cover the pan and let simmer gently until the eggs are fully opaque with runny yolks, about 5 minutes. Cook longer if you prefer your egg yolks to be cooked through.

5. Carefully divide the eggs and sauce between four bowls. Sprinkle about 1 tablespoon crumbled feta over each bowl and serve hot with Greek Village Bread (page 19) or toast.

OMELET THREE WAYS

YIELD: 1 OMELET ▪ TIME: 20 MINUTES ▪ V (CALIFORNIA AND GREEK OMELETS ONLY), GF

A diner is a quester's best friend, especially if your journey takes you across America. While every diner is unique, you can almost always count on their breakfast menus to include omelets. Some eateries have their own signature versions, and many offer regional specialties. Percy, Annabeth, and I each uncovered new favorite takes on this classic breakfast while we were traveling together. These are just a few of the regional omelets you might run into if you happen to be on a quest from New York City to California searching for a stolen lightning bolt of unimaginable power to prevent a war between the gods. Or if you just happen to pop into a diner on a run-of-the-mill road trip, I guess.

OMELET BASE:
3 large eggs
Pinch kosher salt
Pepper to taste

DENVER-STYLE FILLING:
1 tablespoon olive oil
¼ cup diced onions
¼ cup diced bell pepper
¼ cup diced ham

DENVER-STYLE FINISH:
1 tablespoon unsalted butter
2 slices cheddar cheese

CALIFORNIA-STYLE FILLING:
1 tablespoon olive oil
½ cup mixed mushrooms, sliced
¼ cup grape tomatoes, quartered

CALIFORNIA-STYLE FINISH:
1 tablespoon unsalted butter
2 slices cheddar cheese
½ ripe avocado, pitted and sliced, to serve

GREEK-STYLE FILLING:
1 tablespoon olive oil
1 cup baby spinach leaves
¼ cup grape tomatoes, quartered
1 tablespoon kalamata olives, pitted and sliced

GREEK-STYLE FINISH:
1 tablespoon unsalted butter
2 tablespoons crumbled feta cheese

---

1. **TO MAKE THE OMELET BASE:** In a small bowl, beat the eggs and salt together until frothy with no streaks of unincorporated egg white. Set aside.

2. **TO MAKE THE OMELET FILLING OF YOUR CHOICE:** Heat 1 tablespoon of olive oil in an 8-inch nonstick skillet over medium heat until it is just beginning to shimmer. Add the regional filling ingredients and cook, stirring occasionally, until the vegetables soften, 3 to 5 minutes. Season to taste with salt and pepper.

3. To finish each omelet, add 1 tablespoon of butter to your skillet of filling ingredients. Cook until the butter is melted and foaming, then decrease the heat to medium-low. Add the eggs and cook, stirring constantly, until the eggs start to set. Spread the eggs and filling in an even layer, then cover the skillet and cook until the eggs are almost completely set, 2 to 4 minutes longer. Top the eggs and filling with cheese, cover for 30 seconds longer, then remove from heat.

4. Fold the omelet in half, slide onto a plate, and serve. For the California omelet, top with the sliced avocado.

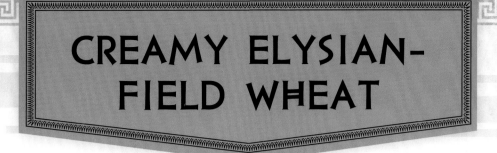

CREAMY ELYSIAN-FIELD WHEAT

YIELD: 4 SERVINGS ▪ TIME: 10 MINUTES ▪ V

The Fields of Elysium are the only part of Hades's realm that doesn't make me feel, well, awful? Terrified? Like running in literally any direction as long as it's away from the Underworld? All of the above, honestly. Elysium is where good souls go after they've passed and, if you're especially heroic, you could end up on the Isles of the Blest. I don't know if they grow wheat in Elysium, but if they do, I bet it could magically turn into a steaming bowl of this creamy wheat cereal if you wanted it to. I'm in no rush to head to the Underworld to test this theory, though. All I know is that a warm bowl of this sweet, lightly spiced breakfast porridge is like a little taste of paradise. And that's good enough for me.

3 cups water
2 cups milk (of your preference)
½ teaspoon kosher salt

2 tablespoons sugar
2 tablespoons honey, plus more for serving

½ teaspoon cinnamon, plus more for serving
1 cup creamy wheat cereal (also known as farina)

1. Combine the water, milk, salt, sugar, honey, and cinnamon in a medium saucepan. Bring to a simmer over medium heat, then stir in the wheat cereal.

2. Cook, stirring constantly to keep the cereal from clumping, until creamy and thickened, about 5 minutes. Remove the pan from the heat.

3. Divide the porridge evenly between four bowls and serve with additional honey and cinnamon to taste.

CHAPTER THREE

LUNCH: THE FORK IN THE ROAD

It sure seems like most quests have a pivotal moment somewhere in the middle that requires a major choice to be made. At least, when I think about the ones I've been a part of . . . That choice can change the trajectory of your journey (for better or worse . . . hopefully better). And it can have a lasting impact on you and your companions. Just like lunch! Personally, I like the fact that around the middle of the day, most folks deliberate about the same thing: what to eat. What you choose CAN have an effect on the rest of your day, but there really are no wrong choices—especially in this chapter. Actually, that's not true. There is a wrong choice to be made, and that's to SKIP LUNCH. Why on earth would you do that? If I had my way, I'd choose TWO lunches!

PEANUT BUTTER AND BANANA-KETCHUP SANDWICH

YIELD: 1 SANDWICH ▪ TIME: 25 MINUTES ▪ V, V+

A certain someone WHO SHALL REMAIN NAMELESS made my experience at Yancy Academy really unpleasant when they threw pieces of their banana-and-ketchup sandwiches at me. Not fun, right? But then I caught a whiff of one of the pieces that bonked me on the head, and I couldn't help myself—I had a taste. That's when I realized this was no ordinary ketchup. The sandwich was made with BANANA ketchup, which I found out is a common condiment from the Philippines. I still don't know how this NAMELESS Yancy student discovered it, and I can't speak to the combination of peanut butter with traditional tomato ketchup, but peanut butter and BANANA ketchup is really good. Banana and peanut butter is already a great combo—a certain king of rock and roll taught us that. Add in some aromatic spices and the sweet-sour-salty combo of vinegar, sugar, and soy sauce, and you've got yourself a real winner.

BANANA KETCHUP:
- 2 tablespoons neutral oil
- 1 small onion, finely chopped
- 1 tablespoon freshly grated ginger
- 1 garlic clove, minced
- ¾ teaspoon ground turmeric
- ¼ teaspoon ground allspice
- ¼ teaspoon sweet paprika
- Pinch ground cloves
- Pinch cayenne pepper
- 4 bananas, mashed
- ½ cup coconut vinegar or distilled white vinegar
- ⅓ cup coconut sugar or light brown sugar
- 1 tablespoon light soy sauce
- ¼ cup water

SANDWICH:
- 2 slices sandwich bread
- 2 tablespoons peanut butter
- 2 tablespoons Banana Ketchup (ingredients above)

1. **TO MAKE THE BANANA KETCHUP:** Heat the oil in a large saucepan over medium-high heat. Add the onions and cook, stirring occasionally, until the onions soften and begin to turn brown on the edges, 7 to 10 minutes.

2. Add the ginger, garlic, turmeric, allspice, paprika, cloves, and cayenne. Cook, stirring constantly, until fragrant, about 1 minute longer.

3. Add the bananas, vinegar, sugar, soy sauce, and water. Cook, stirring occasionally, until the mixture starts to bubble. Lower the heat to a simmer and cook until the mixture is thickened and reduced, 5 to 7 minutes. Remove the pan from the heat and allow the mixture to cool slightly.

4. Using an immersion blender, standard blender, or food processor, blend the mixture until it is smooth. Transfer to a container with a lid and let it cool to room temperature. Keep ketchup refrigerated in an airtight container for up to 1 to 2 weeks.

5. **TO MAKE THE SANDWICH:** Spread the peanut butter on one slice of bread. Top with 2 tablespoons of the banana ketchup and the remaining slice of bread.

GRILLED CHICKEN GYROS

YIELD: 4 SERVINGS ▪ TIME: 1 HOUR 20 MINUTES

Did you know that the Greek gyro (meaning ROUND) was first created in the 1950s by Greek immigrants in the United States? The original recipe involved pork or beef cooked on a spit, then sliced and marinated in vinegar, oregano, and garlic. The meat was placed on a warm pita and rolled up with cool tomatoes, onions, and tzatziki sauce. And sometimes fries. Ideally fries. Today, the term GYRO is sometimes used generically for any kind of cooked protein wrapped in a pita with other fillings. In this recipe's case, we're using grilled chicken that's been marinated in lemon, herbs, and spices. They're great when you're on the go, like Percy, Annabeth, and I always seem to be.

GRILLED CHICKEN:
2 pounds skinless, boneless chicken thighs
Juice and zest of 1 lemon
2 tablespoons oregano leaves
4 garlic cloves, peeled
¼ cup olive oil (preferably Greek), plus more for greasing pan

1½ teaspoon kosher salt
1 teaspoon ground coriander
½ teaspoon ground cumin
½ teaspoon freshly ground black pepper

GYROS:
4 large pitas
2 pounds Grilled Chicken (ingredients above)
Romaine lettuce, chopped
1 cup cherry tomatoes, sliced
Tzatziki (page 72)

1. **TO MAKE THE GRILLED CHICKEN:** Place the chicken thighs in a lidded container or resealable plastic bag. Combine the lemon juice and zest, oregano, garlic, olive oil, salt, coriander, cumin, and black pepper to a food processor or blender. Blend until smooth, then pour the marinade over the chicken, tossing to coat evenly. Seal the container or bag, and chill for at least 1 hour and up to 6.

2. Drain the marinade and use paper towels to pat the chicken dry. Set the chicken thighs on a clean platter.

3. Heat 1 tablespoon of olive oil in a large skillet over medium-high heat until shimmering. Working in batches, lay ⅓ to ½ of the chicken thighs in a single layer on the skillet. Be sure not to overcrowd the pan. Let cook, undisturbed, until well-browned, about 5 to 7 minutes.

4. Flip the chicken thighs and cook for 5 minutes longer, or until an instant-read thermometer registers 165°F when inserted into the thickest part of the chicken. Transfer the cooked chicken to a plate, tent a sheet of foil over it, and keep in a warm place while you cook the remaining chicken.

5. **TO MAKE THE GYROS:** Wipe out the skillet and return it to the stove. Heat the pitas in the skillet until warmed through and pliable, about 1 minute on each side. Set pitas aside in a warm spot.

6. Chop the grilled chicken thighs into bite-size pieces. Divide the chicken between the pitas and fill each as desired with chopped romaine lettuce and tomatoes. Drizzle tzatziki on the chicken and veggies, roll up the gyro into a cone shape, and serve.

AUNTY EM'S DOUBLE SMASH BURGER

YIELD: 4 SERVINGS ▪ TIME: 1 HOUR 30 MINUTES

Our first quest got off to a rocky start . . . literally! Something about Aunty Em's Gnome Emporium didn't sit well with me, but try telling that to a kind-hearted and hungry Percy when there's a welcoming host and a pile of cheeseburgers in front of him. Trust me, you don't want to get between that guy and food, especially if it's a burger. Still, we knew something was up with that Aunty Em. You know, like the fact that she was the gorgon Medusa! Thank goodness Percy had me and Annabeth with him; otherwise, his quest would've had a rocky start AND end. Just like my poor Uncle Ferdinand. These burgers represent one of the only good parts about stopping at Aunty Em's. They're even topped with snake-like caramelized onions to really drive the point home. A little on-the-nose if you ask me, but Percy and Annabeth seem to like them.

CARAMELIZED ONIONS:

4 tablespoons neutral oil

1 pound yellow onions, peeled, ends trimmed, sliced to ¼-inch-thick rounds

1 teaspoon kosher salt

1 teaspoon freshly ground black pepper

½ teaspoon dried thyme

1 tablespoon red wine vinegar

SMASH BURGERS:

1 pound ground beef

Kosher salt

Freshly ground black pepper

8 slices American cheese

4 hamburger buns

Caramelized Onions (ingredients above)

1. **TO MAKE THE CARAMELIZED ONIONS:** Heat the oil in a large Dutch oven or heavy-bottomed pot over medium-high heat until it begins to shimmer. Add the onions and season with the salt and pepper. Cook the onions, stirring occasionally, until softened, about 5 to 7 minutes.

2. Reduce the heat to medium, and cook for about 1 hour, stirring occasionally, until the onions are a deep golden brown and very soft. If the pan starts to look dry, add a splash of water (about 2 tablespoons), and scrape up any browned bits of fond at the bottom of the Dutch oven. Repeat as often as necessary throughout the cooking process. Once the onions are soft and golden brown, stir in the thyme and red wine vinegar and cook just until the liquid has evaporated, about 2 to 4 minutes longer. Caramelized onions may be made up to 1 week in advance and stored in an airtight container in the fridge.

3. **TO MAKE THE BURGERS:** Divide the ground beef into eight 2-ounce portions, shaping each into a ball. Set aside on a platter.

4. Heat a griddle over medium-high heat—once the heat radiating from the griddle feels quite hot when you hover your hand a couple inches above it, you're ready to go.

5. Place as many of the portions of ground beef as you can (keeping in mind that you're about to smash them out to about 3- to 4-inch-wide patties) on the griddle. Using a flat, metal spatula, press down on each patty until it's very flat and thin, just a bit wider than your burger buns. Season them with a pinch each of salt and pepper. Let cook, undisturbed, until they are crisp and deeply browned, about 3 minutes. Scrape the burger patties up with the spatula (they will stick to the griddle somewhat), flip them, top them with cheese, and cook for about 1 minute longer.

6. Transfer the cooked burgers to the buns, using two patties per bun, and top with as much of the caramelized onions as you like. Repeat with the remaining burgers.

GREEK SALAD

YIELD: 4 SERVINGS ▪ TIME: 15 MINUTES ▪ V, GF

Traditionally, a Greek salad is made with very few ingredients. You can usually count on a classic version to have cucumbers, tomatoes, red onions, olives, and feta. There's a time and a place to mess with convention (trust me, Percy and I are no strangers to breaking a few rules here and there, and even Annabeth has been known to let things slide on occasion), but we're choosing to stick to tradition with this salad, for no other reason than we like it just the way it is. If you want to add some other things yourself, go for it! Mix it up with some chopped romaine or other crunchy lettuce and throw in other vegetables to your hearts' content. I won't tell the Kindly Ones, I promise. The salad is best made the day you plan on eating it, but the dressing can be made up to a week in advance.

DRESSING:
¼ cup red wine vinegar

½ teaspoon dried oregano

½ teaspoon kosher salt

¼ teaspoon freshly
ground black pepper

½ cup olive oil
(preferably Greek)

SALAD:
1 English cucumber,
peeled, halved sliced
to ½-inch half-moons

3 cups assorted cherry and
grape tomatoes, halved

¼ small red onion,
very thinly sliced

½ cup kalamata olives

8 ounces feta cheese, drained
and sliced

1. **TO MAKE THE DRESSING:** In a medium bowl, whisk together the vinegar, oregano, salt, and pepper until the salt has dissolved. While whisking constantly, pour the olive oil into the bowl in a steady, thin stream. Set aside.

2. **TO MAKE THE SALAD:** Toss the cucumbers, tomatoes, onions, and olives together in a serving bowl. Top with slices of feta. Serve with the dressing on the side.

APOLLO'S OFFERING
(FASOLADA)

YIELD: 4 TO 6 SERVINGS • TIME: 1 HOUR 30 MINUTES • V, V+, GF

It's been said that, back in ancient Greece, Athenians made this vegetarian soup as an offering to Apollo during the Pyanopsia Festival (PYANOPSIA even means BEAN-STEWING/BOILING). It is still a Greek staple to this day. As with many traditional dishes, each household makes it a little bit differently—you could say there are as many versions of fasolada as there are families in Greece, and that would not be much of an exaggeration. This is as close to the version favored by the campers in Cabin 7 as we could make, and it goes really well with a nice crusty slice of Greek Village Bread (page 19). To cut way down on the cooking time, I suggest soaking the beans overnight. Or you can skip the dried beans altogether and just use precooked, canned beans. Nobody's above taking a little shortcut or two, right? Either way, you'll end up with a tasty bowl of soup.

1 pound dried white beans, like navy or great northern

2 quarts water

2 tablespoons olive oil

4 large carrots, peeled and cut into ¼-inch-thick coins

3 celery stalks, diced

1 medium onion, chopped

1 teaspoon kosher salt

½ teaspoon freshly ground black pepper

¼ cup tomato paste

4 garlic cloves, minced

1 teaspoon dried oregano

½ teaspoon dried thyme

1 bay leaf

2 quarts low-sodium vegetable stock

You can also use 2 cans of drained white beans instead of these first two ingredients. —Annabeth

1. Place the beans in a large bowl, along with 2 quarts of water. Cover the bowl and let the beans soak for at least 8 hours or overnight. When you're ready to cook, drain the beans and discard the soaking liquid. If you're using canned beans, skip this step.

2. Heat the olive oil in a large Dutch oven or heavy-bottomed pot over medium-high heat until shimmering. Add the carrots, celery, and onion to the pot and season with salt and pepper. Cook, stirring frequently, until the vegetables are softened, about 7 to 10 minutes.

3. Add the tomato paste and cook, stirring constantly, until it has darkened to a deep brick-red color, about 3 to 5 minutes. Add the garlic and cook, stirring constantly, for 1 minute longer. Add the soaked beans (do not add the beans yet if you are using precooked canned beans), oregano, thyme, bay leaf, and vegetable stock.

4. Bring the soup to a boil, then reduce to a simmer. Cover the pot and let the fasolada cook, stirring occasionally, until the beans are tender and creamy, 45 to 60 minutes. If using canned beans, instead simmer the vegetables for just 30 minutes, then add the beans and simmer for 15 minutes longer.

5. Season the soup to taste with salt and pepper. Serve hot with crusty bread.

ORZO AND GRILLED HALLOUMI SALAD
WITH POMEGRANATE DRESSING

YIELD: 4 SERVINGS ▪ TIME: 30 MINUTES ▪ V

One of the most fascinating spots in the Underworld is Persephone's Garden. It's full of strange and interesting plants, which are cool to look at but best left alone—I know that much from experience. I'm just grateful Annabeth and Percy were with me, because the pomegranates in that place are some of the most beautiful and tempting this satyr has ever seen. Turns out, if you eat one, you kinda . . . BECOME part of the garden, and I did not sign up for that. Although Persephone wasn't around when we met with Hades (things might have gone a little smoother if she had been), we want to honor her and her beautiful garden with this salad made with pomegranate dressing. Just make sure to get your pomegranate molasses from the store and not the Underworld, okay?

DRESSING:
2 tablespoons pomegranate molasses

1 tablespoon honey

1 tablespoon freshly squeezed lemon juice

¼ teaspoon kosher salt

½ cup olive oil

2 teaspoons fresh mint leaves, minced

SALAD:
1 large zucchini, ends trimmed and quartered lengthwise

1 yellow summer squash, ends trimmed and quartered lengthwise

2 tablespoons olive oil, divided

8 ounces halloumi, drained and patted dry

1 cup orzo, cooked and cooled

4 cups baby spinach, coarsely chopped

1 large cucumber, peeled and large diced

1 cup grape tomatoes, halved

1. **TO MAKE THE DRESSING:** In a small bowl, whisk the pomegranate molasses, honey, lemon juice, and salt together until the salt has dissolved. Whisking constantly, pour in the olive oil in a thin, steady stream until the dressing is emulsified and smooth. Stir in the mint leaves and set aside.

2. **TO MAKE THE SALAD:** Preheat the broiler in your oven. Line a half-sheet pan with foil. Brush the zucchini and yellow summer squash with 1 tablespoon of the olive oil. Season lightly with salt and pepper. Cook under the broiler until deeply golden brown and tender—the time this takes will vary depending on the strength of your broiler, but 5 to 10 minutes is a rough estimate. Check frequently after the 3-minute mark. Set aside to cool once cooked.

3. Heat the remaining olive oil in a skillet over medium-high heat until shimmering. Fry the halloumi in the oil until it's golden brown, about 3 to 5 minutes. Flip the halloumi and cook it for 3 to 5 minutes longer. Set aside to cool.

4. Once they are all cool enough to handle, chop the zucchini, yellow summer squash, and halloumi into bite-size pieces.

5. In a large bowl, toss the orzo, spinach, cucumber, tomatoes, and prepared zucchini, yellow summer squash, and halloumi together until well-distributed. Serve with the prepared dressing.

MANESTRA

YIELD: 2 TO 4 SERVINGS ▪ TIME: 25 MINUTES ▪ V (IF USING VEGETABLE STOCK)

Any food can be a comfort food if it makes you feel good and, well, comforted, right? This Greek soup is super easy to make and definitely fits the bill. It's a simple tomato soup with orzo in it. As the orzo cooks, the starch soaks into the broth to give it a slightly thicker, stewlike consistency. It's great as is, but this version tops it off with a little bit of salty, briny feta for extra flavor. I've heard that this is the kind of thing Sally Jackson might make for Percy when he's home sick from school. These days, it's also great for a midday break when we're questing during cold or rainy weather. Chiron's been known to suggest this as a meal for heroes after a particularly rough day of training, or when the occasional impossible storm occurs over a camp where it never seems to rain . . .

2 tablespoons olive oil
1 small onion, minced
4 garlic cloves, minced
1½ teaspoons dried oregano
One 28-ounce can whole peeled plum tomatoes

1 teaspoon kosher salt
½ teaspoon freshly ground black pepper
4 cups chicken stock (or vegetable stock to keep it vegetarian)

1 cup orzo
1 bay leaf
Crumbled feta cheese, for garnish

1. Heat the oil in a medium saucepan over medium-high heat until shimmering. Add the onions and cook, stirring occasionally, until they are softened, 5 to 7 minutes.

2. Add the garlic and cook, stirring constantly, until fragrant, about 1 minute longer.

3. Add the oregano and tomatoes to the saucepan. Season with salt and pepper. Mash the tomatoes with the back of a spoon, or a potato masher, until the mixture turns into a chunky sauce.

4. Stir in the chicken or vegetable stock. At this point, if you prefer the broth to be smooth, use an immersion blender to blend until smooth, or blend in batches using a standard blender. Bring the mixture to a boil, then stir in the orzo and bay leaf. Cook, stirring frequently to keep the orzo from clumping, until the orzo is tender, about 10 minutes.

5. Remove and discard the bay leaf, then serve the soup with crumbled feta.

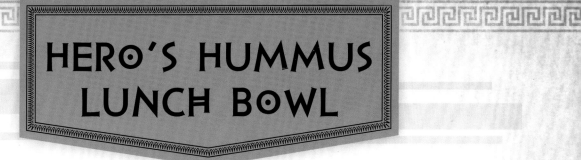

HERO'S HUMMUS LUNCH BOWL

YIELD: 4 TO 6 SERVINGS • TIME: 20 MINUTES • GF

I'm the first to admit that I have a tendency to snack when I'm nervous. As someone who's run into Kindly Ones, been in the presence of the most powerful gods in the pantheon, and encountered Medusa, I think I've had entirely fair reasons to gnaw on a tin can or two . . . or our food reserves. And maybe, just maybe, it has happened once or twice that come lunchtime all we've got left are a smattering of disconnected scraps. Fortunately, Annabeth has a good head on her shoulders, and on those occasions she has reminded us that leftovers can make a meal—they just need a little something to bring them all together. In this case, we start with a base of freshly made hummus and top it with whatever bits and bobs we've got. The hummus provides all the protein I need, but you could top it with any cooked protein and raw or cooked vegetables you like. Or just skip the bowl concept entirely and enjoy the hummus as a dip on its own.

HUMMUS:
Two 15½-ounce cans chickpeas
⅓ cup tahini
Juice of 2 lemons
1¼ teaspoon kosher salt
2 garlic cloves, minced

1 teaspoon ground coriander
1 teaspoon ground cumin
¼ cup olive oil
2 tablespoons chickpea liquid, plus more if needed

HUMMUS BOWL TOPPINGS:
Greek Salad (page 51)
Grilled Halloumi Salad (page 55)
Souvlaki (page 71)
Chicken from Grilled Chicken Gyros (page 47)

1. **TO MAKE THE HUMMUS:** Drain the chickpeas, reserving the liquid from the can. Transfer the chickpeas to the bowl of a food processor.

2. Add the tahini, lemon juice, salt, garlic, coriander, and cumin. Pulse until smooth, scraping down the sides of the food processor bowl as needed.

3. With the food processor running, add the olive oil in a slow, steady stream until it is fully incorporated. Repeat this process with 2 tablespoons of the chickpea liquid. Stop the food processor and check the consistency and seasoning of the hummus. If it is too thick, add 1 tablespoon more of the chickpea liquid. Add more salt if needed.

4. **TO MAKE HUMMUS BOWL:** Spread about ½ cup hummus in the bottom of a wide, shallow bowl. Top with leftovers. You can use the listed toppings or substitute any cooked grains, cooked or raw vegetables, prepared protein, or extra salad—customize to your liking.

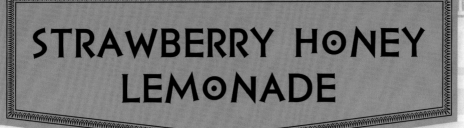

STRAWBERRY HONEY LEMONADE

YIELD: ABOUT 1½ QUARTS ▪ TIME: 10 MINUTES ▪ V, GF

Have I mentioned that it (almost) never rains at Camp Half-Blood? Really! It's one of the reasons we're able to keep a year-round strawberry farm in business. That, and the fact that Mr. D is pretty legendary when it comes to growing fruit. On your own quest, it may not ALWAYS feel like summer. But when it does, this lemonade is about as thirst-quenching as they come. Mr. D's actually the one who suggested honey instead of sugar. I think it may have been a peace-making gesture for Zeus, especially after that one storm . . . From what I understand, Zeus was raised on milk and honey. Then again, it adds just the right amount of sweetness to this recipe and maybe that's all there is to it.

1 cup fresh-squeezed
lemon juice

½ cup honey
2 cups chopped strawberries

½ vanilla bean (optional)
1 quart cold water

This may require 6 to 10 lemons. —Annabeth

1. Pour the lemon juice, honey, and strawberries into a blender. If using vanilla bean, scrape seeds into the mix. Blend until smooth.

2. Pour the mixture into a bowl over a fine-mesh strainer to strain out any solids. Use a rubber spatula to help push the liquid through the strainer.

3. Pour strained mixture into a pitcher and add cold water. Stir, pour over ice, and enjoy!

SEAWEED SALAD

YIELD: 4 SERVINGS ▪ TIME: 20 MINUTES ▪ V

You won't see Percy eating this salad when Annabeth's around. He wouldn't risk a new nickname like "Seaweed Guts." But that doesn't mean he doesn't enjoy it on his own, offering a little to the firepit for his father first. I don't want to stick my hoof in where it doesn't belong, so I won't speculate further. What I WILL do is note that this is a particularly flavorful recipe, one ideal for heroes looking for a lunch on the saltier side. It might even make you feel a little closer to the ocean, yourself . . .

On the playful names I've given Percy since we met, no comment. On the salad, it's worth mentioning that dried wakame, a kind of kelp, is sometimes easier to find than seaweed salad mix, but it works just as well for this recipe. —Annabeth

SALAD:
1 ounce dried seaweed salad mix or dried wakame (about ¾ cup)

6 cups cold water

2 mini cucumbers, thinly sliced

1 medium carrot, peeled and shredded

DRESSING:
1 tablespoon white miso

1 tablespoon soy sauce

1 tablespoon rice vinegar

1 tablespoon toasted sesame oil

2 teaspoons mirin

2 teaspoons grated ginger

1 teaspoon maple syrup

1 tablespoon roasted white sesame seeds, plus more for topping

1. **TO MAKE THE SALAD:** In a medium bowl, combine the dried seaweed or dried wakame with 6 cups of cold water. Cover the bowl and let soak in the refrigerator for about 10 minutes, until fully rehydrated. Drain seaweed or wakame in a colander, squeezing out the excess water with your hands.

2. If the seaweed or wakame pieces are quite large, give them a rough chop on a cutting board for more bite-size pieces—don't worry about making them uniform. Transfer them to a serving bowl along with the cucumber and carrot. Cover the bowl and chill in the fridge until ready to serve.

3. **TO MAKE THE DRESSING:** Stir together the miso, soy sauce, rice vinegar, sesame oil, mirin, ginger, and maple syrup in a small bowl until smooth. Stir in the sesame seeds.

4. Add the dressing to the salad mix and toss to coat. Divide the salad evenly among four small salad bowls, sprinkle with more sesame seeds, and serve.

CHAPTER FOUR

APPETIZERS: THE BEGINNING OF THE END

It's not exactly a secret that I love eating, so let me tell you that when I learned about the concept of the APPETIZER, I couldn't have been happier. Food you eat to get yourself ready for a meal? What a concept! Now some of these recipes could be meals in and of themselves, if you were to help yourself to a large portion—that's something I've been known to do on occasion without any guilt whatsoever. For example, it'd be pretty easy to make a meal of Sally Jackson's Seven-Layer Dip. Or you could make a few of the different dishes you'd find on a meze platter, like htipiti or marinated olives, and make a whole meal of that. In either case, I consider it an important responsibility to prepare yourself for the final meal of the day, or the final hurdle on your quest.

SALLY JACKSON'S SEVEN-LAYER DIP

YIELD: 6 TO 8 SERVINGS • TIME: 45 MINUTES • V*, V+*, GF

This oft-requested appetizer (and REQUESTED is putting it nicely) is a Sally Jackson specialty. She starts with a layer of well-seasoned ground beef, followed by refried beans, cheese, guacamole, salsa, sour cream, and finishes with sliced olives. It goes best with tortilla chips, especially if they're made with blue corn masa (well, that's according to Percy, but really any tortilla chips will do). You can make your own blue corn tortilla chips (page 69) if you're up to the task, but store-bought chips are perfectly fine. This recipe makes a decent amount of dip, so it's good for a crowd. Enough, say, for a poker night or, even better, to celebrate a big art sale. You can serve this dish warm right after you make it, or you can make and chill the individual elements ahead of time to serve it, like revenge, nice and cold.

MEAT LAYER:
- 2 teaspoons ancho chile powder
- 1 teaspoon kosher salt
- 1 teaspoon cornstarch
- 1 teaspoon ground cumin
- 1 teaspoon onion powder
- ½ teaspoon garlic powder
- ½ teaspoon freshky ground black pepper
- ½ teaspoon ground coriander
- ½ teaspoon Mexican oregano
- 1 tablespoon olive oil
- 1 pound ground beef
- 2 tablespoons tomato paste
- 1 cup water

A plant-based meat substitute could work here, so long as you follow the package instructions. —Annabeth

SALSA LAYER:
- 1 small onion, peeled and roughly chopped
- 1 jalapeño, stemmed and roughly chopped
- 1 pound Roma tomatoes, cored and roughly chopped
- ¼ cup cilantro leaves and tender stems
- Juice of 2 limes
- 1 tablespoon olive oil
- ½ teaspoon kosher salt

GUACAMOLE LAYER:
- 4 ripe medium avocados, halved and pitted
- ½ teaspoon kosher salt
- Juice of 1 lime

SEVEN-LAYER DIP:
- 1 can refried pinto beans
- Meat Layer (ingredients above)
- 1½ cups shredded cheddar Jack cheese
- Guacamole Layer (ingredients above)
- Salsa Layer (ingredients above)
- ½ cup sour cream
- One 2¼-ounce can sliced black olives, drained
- Blue Corn Tortilla Chips (page 69), for serving

1. **TO MAKE THE MEAT LAYER:** In a small bowl, whisk together the chile powder, salt, cornstarch, cumin, onion powder, garlic powder, pepper, coriander, and oregano. Heat the oil in a large skillet over medium-high heat until it's shimmering.

2. Add the ground beef to the skillet and cook, breaking the meat apart with a wooden spoon, until well-browned and cooked through, 7 to 10 minutes. Drain any excess fat, then add the tomato paste. Cook, stirring constantly, until the tomato paste has slightly darkened, about 3 minutes. Add the spice mixture and the water. Cook, stirring occasionally, until most of the liquid has evaporated, 5 to 8 minutes. Remove the skillet from the heat and set aside. (If you're serving the dip cold, let the meat layer cool before transferring it to an airtight container and chilling it in the fridge.)

3. **TO MAKE THE SALSA LAYER:** Add all the salsa ingredients to the bowl of a food processor. Pulse until a chunky sauce forms. Season to taste with additional salt or lime juice if desired. Set the salsa aside or, if you're serving the dish cold, transfer to a separate airtight container and chill it in the fridge.

4. **TO MAKE THE GUACAMOLE LAYER:** Scoop the avocado flesh into a medium bowl and discard the skins. Season with salt and lime juice, then mash the avocado with a fork to your preferred consistency.

5. **TO MAKE THE SEVEN-LAYER-DIP:** If you plan to serve the dish warm, put refried beans in a microwave-safe bowl, cover it with a damp paper towel, and microwave for 90 seconds. Stir the beans, then microwave for 1 minute longer. Spoon the meat layer into the bottom of a 2-quart baking dish, casserole tray, or serving bowl. Spoon the refried beans over the meat layer, followed by the cheese.

6. Spread the guacamole over the cheese layer, leaving an outer ring of cheese exposed. From this point, make each remaining layer a little smaller so that a ring of the previous layer is exposed. Top the guacamole with the remaining layers in the following order: salsa, sour cream, and black olives. Serve with tortilla chips.

BLUE CORN TORTILLA CHIPS

YIELD: 6 TO 8 SERVINGS ▪ TIME: 45 MINUTES ▪ V, V+, GF

White and yellow corn chips are pretty common, but red and blue varieties are rarer, though definitely easier to find than the great god Pan. I'm only being a little SATYRical here (see, that's a satyr joke). So, naturally, whenever Sally Jackson needs to make her famous Seven Layer Dip, she whips up a batch of blue corn tortilla chips just for Percy. Of course, you can't make tortilla chips without first making tortillas, which makes this recipe just a little self-serving, since you need tortillas for my very favorite Bean-and-Cheese Enchiladas (page 94), too. Of course, store-bought will work just fine. But there's something gratifying about making your own tortillas and chips. It's not that hard, AND they usually taste better. That's what I call a win-win (and can't we all use more of those?).

---

1 cup warm water

½ teaspoon kosher salt, plus more to taste for chip seasoning

1 cup blue corn masa

2 quarts neutral oil, such as canola, corn, or peanut, for frying

---

1. **TO MAKE THE TORTILLAS:** In a small bowl, stir the water and ½ teaspoon salt together in a bowl until the salt dissolves. Add the masa and mix until a soft dough forms. It should be very slightly tacky, but not sticky—if it's sticky, that means it's too wet and you'll need to add a bit more masa, 1 tablespoon at a time, until the right consistency is reached. Conversely, if it's too dry and crumbly, add a bit more water, 1 tablespoon at a time. Cover the dough and set it aside.

2. Open a quart-size zip-top plastic bag. Cut the side seams with a sharp knife or scissors, leaving the bottom seam intact—you'll use this to line the tortilla press. Heat a griddle over medium heat.

3. Shape the dough into walnut-size balls. Flatten the dough balls one at a time using a tortilla press lined with the prepared plastic bag. Press down on the lever once, then rotate the tortilla 180° and lightly press again. Peel the tortilla from the plastic bag and gently lay it on the griddle. Cook the tortilla for 1 minute on each side, then transfer it to a wire rack to cool. Repeat with the remaining masa dough portions.

If you don't have a tortilla press, use a perfectly flat-bottomed, heavy skillet (put that cast-iron skillet to work) to flatten the tortillas. —Annabeth

4. **TO MAKE THE TORTILLA CHIPS:** Stack the tortillas on a cutting board in two stacks. Cut the stacks into wedges (6 to 8 wedges per tortilla, depending on how large you like your chips). Set aside.

5. Line a half-sheet pan with paper towels. Heat 2 quarts of oil in a deep fryer or large Dutch oven to 350°F, using a candy thermometer or instant-read thermometer to measure the temperature. Carefully add about ¼ of the tortilla wedges to the hot oil. Cook, stirring occasionally with a slotted metal spoon or wire-mesh spider scoop, until the tortilla wedges are a few shades darker, 2 to 3 minutes. Blue corn masa chips present a bit of a challenge since they won't turn the same golden color as standard masa chips when they're finished cooking. The cook time is fairly reliable, but if you're still unsure, pay attention to the oil. The chips will make the oil bubble up quite a bit when you first add them and as they cook—you'll know they're just about done when the bubbling slows way down.

6. Transfer the chips to the prepared half-sheet pan and season them to taste with salt while they're still hot. Repeat the process with the remaining tortilla wedges. Store leftover chips in an airtight container at room temperature for up to 3 days.

SOUVLAKI

(AKA SKEWERED MINOTAUR)

YIELD: 4 SERVINGS ▪ TIME: 1 HOUR 20 MINUTES ▪ GF

Souvlaki is one of those classic Greek dishes that can come prepared a bunch of different ways. One constant is the skewer, but the meat can be anything you like. In Greece, pork is the most common, but you can also make souvlaki with chicken, lamb, or beef (feel free to swap any of those meats in for the pork in this recipe). PERSASSY likes to joke that this dish should be called Skewered Minotaur since he defeated Asterion by, well, SKEWERING him with his own horn. But please, please don't encourage him with that one. It makes me nervous enough that he uses the Kindly Ones' names at all. They do not take KINDLY to being mocked . . .

1 pound pork tenderloin, cut into 1-inch cubes	3 garlic cloves, peeled	½ teaspoon fresh rosemary leaves
¼ cup olive oil	1 teaspoon kosher salt	½ teaspoon fresh oregano leaves
1 tablespoon honey	1 teaspoon fresh thyme leaves	
Juice and zest of 1 lemon	½ teaspoon freshly ground black pepper	Bamboo skewers (not Minotaur horns)

1. Place the pork in a resealable plastic bag or a medium bowl. Combine the oil, honey, lemon zest and juice, garlic, salt, thyme, pepper, rosemary, and oregano in the bowl of a food processor. Pulse to combine, about 1 to 2 minutes.

2. Pour the marinade all over the pork, massaging the bag (or tossing the meat in the bowl) to ensure even coverage. Seal the container and refrigerate for at least 1 hour or up to 8 hours.

3. Thread 4 to 6 pieces of marinated meat onto each skewer until you've used up all of the meat. Heat a grill or broiler on high. Cook the meat on the grill or under the broiler, rotating the skewers every 90 seconds or so, until the meat is well-browned on all sides and cooked through, about 6 to 10 minutes total. Serve immediately.

MARINATED OLIVES

YIELD: ABOUT 2 CUPS • TIME: 1 HOUR 15 MINUTES • V, V+, GF

Olives are plenty tasty on their own—just ask Annabeth, or any of the children of Athena. But the fact that something is already delicious doesn't mean you can't make it even MORE so. Like, I love bean-and-cheese enchiladas, but I bet I'd love them even more with a little freshly grated aluminum can on top (recommended only for satyrs, of course). With a few tasty seasonings—herbs, garlic, and red pepper flakes for a little heat—you can elevate something great to a whole new level! It's a dish you could proudly serve as part of a meze platter for Athena herself. That's what Annabeth would do, anyway.

1 large lemon	1 teaspoon fresh thyme leaves, minced	½ cup olive oil
2 cups mixed olives (castelvetrano and kalamata are great), drained	½ teaspoon fresh oregano leaves, minced	4 garlic cloves, peeled
		¼ teaspoon crushed red pepper flakes

1. Use a sharp knife or peeler to remove 2 or 3 strips of peel from the lemon. Set the strips of peel aside for later. Halve the lemon and squeeze the juice into a medium bowl.

2. Add the olives, thyme, and oregano to the bowl of lemon juice.

3. Combine the strips of lemon peel, olive oil, garlic, and red pepper flakes to a small saucepan. Warm the oil mixture over low heat for 7 to 10 minutes, until it is quite fragrant and the garlic turns just golden on the edges.

4. Pour the warmed oil mixture over the olives and herbs, stir, and let marinate for 1 hour before serving.

TZATZIKI

YIELD: ABOUT 1½ CUPS • TIME: 1 HOUR 15 MINUTES • V, GF

This meze-platter mainstay can also be used as sauce or condiment for many of the dishes throughout this book, like Grilled Chicken Gyros (page 47), Icarus's Melt-in-Your-Mouth Wings (page 73), and Zucchini Fritters (page 85). Traditional recipes use sheep or goat milk Greek yogurt, which is great if you can find some near you—they're both tangier than cow's milk yogurt, giving the final product a unique taste. But if cow's milk Greek yogurt is all you have, your tzatziki will still be delicious. The cooling mint is like a breath of winter, while the bright lemon juice and green cucumbers taste like summer, making this the perfect dish to serve at any solstice gathering, or any time of year, really!

1 cucumber, peeled, ends trimmed (about 8 ounces)	1 cup Greek yogurt	1 garlic clove, finely grated
1 teaspoon kosher salt	2 tablespoons mint leaves, minced	Juice of 1 lemon

1. Shred the cucumber using the larger holes on a box grater. Transfer the shredded cucumber to a colander, then season it with salt.

2. Let the shredded and salted cucumber sit for 10 minutes, then press it against the sides of the colander with your hand to squeeze out the excess moisture. Transfer the cucumber to a bowl.

3. Add the yogurt, mint leaves, garlic, and lemon juice to the bowl. Stir to combine, season with additional salt if needed, then cover and refrigerate for 1 hour before serving.

ICARUS'S MELT-IN-YOUR-MOUTH WINGS

YIELD: 4 TO 6 SERVINGS ▪ TIME: 1 HOUR 40 MINUTES ▪ GF

Oh, Icarus. Son of Daedalus, the great inventor who was a demigod son of Athena. You could have done great things if you hadn't flown so close to the sun. Considering the penchant Percy, Annabeth, and even I (sometimes, sort of) have for biting off more than we can chew when it comes to quests, we thought it would be nice to honor Icarus and his ill-fated wings for the valuable lesson his story imparts (but we don't seem to learn). Percy prefers calling these Fury Wings, but ew—a Fury's wings are like bat wings. Annabeth assures me that these wings are anything but ew. They're coated in a light dressing that features classic Greek flavors, like lemon and oregano, filling each bite with bright and summery goodness. Unlike Icarus's wings, they melt in your mouth, not in the sun. Though I suppose if Helios got mad enough, he could melt anything. Hmm. Probably best not to think about that one too hard.

WINGS:
2 to 3 pounds chicken wings

2 tablespoons olive oil

2 teaspoons kosher salt

2 teaspoons dried oregano

1 teaspoon freshly ground black pepper

Zest of 1 lemon

DRESSING:
¼ cup olive oil

2 tablespoons lemon juice

1 garlic clove, grated

1 tablespoon honey

½ teaspoon kosher salt

¼ teaspoon freshly ground black pepper

¼ teaspoon crushed red pepper flakes

Tzatziki (page 72), for serving (optional)

1. **TO MAKE THE WINGS:** Place the chicken pieces in a large bowl and drizzle olive oil all over them. Season with the salt, oregano, pepper, and lemon zest, tossing the wings to coat them evenly. Cover and refrigerate for at least 1 hour, and up to 12.

2. Preheat the oven to 400°F. Set two oven-safe wire cooling racks into two half-sheet pans. Spray the racks with cooking spray. Spread the wings out in an even layer, spacing them across both racks. Bake for 30 minutes. Then flip the wings, rotate the pans, and bake for 25 to 30 minutes longer, until the wings are golden brown and crisp.

3. **TO MAKE THE DRESSING:** While the wings cook, combine the olive oil, lemon juice, garlic, honey, salt, black pepper, and red pepper flakes in a small bowl and whisk until the honey and salt have dissolved. Set aside.

4. Transfer the cooked wings to a large heat-proof bowl while they are still hot. Pour the dressing all over the wings, then toss them to coat. Serve immediately with tzatziki, if using.

SPANAKOPITA

YIELD: 6 TO 8 SERVINGS • TIME: 2 HOURS • V

Spanakopita (which translates to "spinach pie") can come in many forms. You might see individual hand-pies made of triangular golden envelopes of flaky phyllo pastry filled with spinach, cheese, and herbs. Or you might encounter larger versions that are square, rectangular, or round. The round ones, as in this recipe, remind me of a giant golden drachma. I know drachma are an important part of any quest, in case you need to curry a little favor with a god or even a certain boatsman on the river Styx, but give me some spanakopita over gold coins any day. I can't help but wonder if ol' Charon would give me a ride in exchange for some of this delicious, golden spinach-and-cheese pie. It couldn't hurt to ask, right?

½ cup unsalted butter, melted

2 pounds frozen spinach, thawed

1 tablespoon olive oil

6 scallions, thinly sliced (white and light-green parts only)

1 shallot, minced

4 garlic cloves, minced

¼ teaspoon crushed red pepper flakes

2 tablespoons fresh dill, minced

2 tablespoons fresh oregano, minced

1 tablespoon fresh parsley, minced

2 large eggs, beaten

½ teaspoon kosher salt

½ teaspoon freshly ground black pepper

Pinch freshly grated nutmeg

8 ounces feta cheese, drained and crumbled

¼ cup grated Pecorino Romano cheese

12 sheets phyllo dough, thawed

1. Heat the oven to 375°F. Brush the inside of an 8-inch springform pan with a thin layer of the melted butter. Set aside.

2. Place the spinach on a large, clean kitchen towel. Gather up the sides of the towel, then twist and squeeze it over the sink to drain as much of the excess liquid as you can from the spinach. Transfer the spinach to a large bowl.

3. Heat the oil in a medium skillet over medium-high heat until just shimmering. Add the scallions and shallot and cook, stirring constantly, until they are softened, 3 to 5 minutes.

4. Add the garlic and cook, stirring constantly, for 1 minute longer. Scrape the contents of the skillet, oil and all, into the bowl of spinach.

5. Add the crushed red pepper flakes, dill, oregano, parsley, eggs, salt, pepper, nutmeg, feta, and Pecorino Romano cheese to the bowl of spinach. Stir well to evenly distribute all of the ingredients.

6. Lay the sheets of phyllo dough out on a clean work surface. Cover with a slightly damp kitchen towel to keep the dough from drying out. Working with one sheet at a time, brush the surface of each sheet generously with melted butter. Place the sheet, butter-side up, into the bottom of the prepared springform pan, pressing the excess down around the edges and completely covering the bottom of the pan. Repeat this process with three more sheets of phyllo, layering the phyllo sheets on top of each other.

7. Brush another sheet of phyllo with butter. This time, line the side of the springform pan vertically with the phyllo so that a little bit overlaps with the phyllo at the bottom of the pan. You should end up with a 2- to 3-inch overhang of phyllo over the sides of the pan. Repeat this process with three more sheets of phyllo, overlapping the phyllo and pressing it onto the sides of the pan as you go.

8. Working quickly, fill the pan with the spinach and feta filling, gently pressing down to compact it and spread it evenly.

9. Fold the overhanging phyllo over the top of the filling, letting it crumple and sit unevenly. Brush butter on the remaining two sheets of phyllo, then gently drape and press them down onto the top of the pan, again letting the pastry sit crumpled and unevenly. Brush or drizzle with any remaining butter.

10. Bake the spanakopita for 50 to 75 minutes, until it is deeply golden brown all over. Start checking the pastry at the 50-minute mark as phyllo can burn easily if left to bake for too long. Let the spanakopita cool in the pan before unmolding and serving.

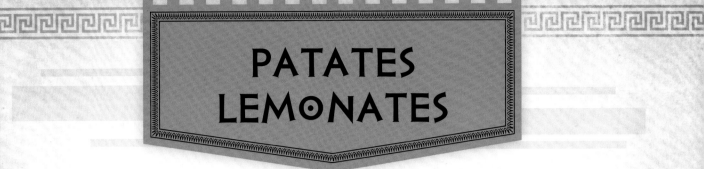

PATATES LEMONATES

YIELD: 4 TO 6 SERVINGS · TIME: 2 HOURS · V, V+ (IF USING VEGETABLE STOCK), GF

There are so many ways to prepare potatoes: boiled, mashed, steamed, roasted, baked, and fried, to name a few. This classic Greek approach combines a few of those methods for potatoes that are creamy on the inside and slightly crisp and super flavorful on the outside. Perhaps because of all the lemon juice used to give these potatoes their signature flavor, Mr. D likes to serve them when he's in a particularly SOUR mood. In other words, we've had them almost daily since Percy arrived at Camp Half-Blood . . . Hmmm. I wonder if there's a correlation . . . The classic preparation uses chicken stock to give the potatoes an extra boost of umami, but you could easily swap that out for vegetable stock to keep these taters satyr-friendly. Whichever type of stock you use, get ready for potatoes packed with lemony, garlicky, herby flavor that'll keep you coming back to this simple side dish.

2 pounds Yukon Gold potatoes, peeled and cut into wedges

⅓ cup olive oil

½ cup low-sodium chicken or vegetable stock

¼ cup lemon juice, plus more for serving

4 garlic cloves, grated

1½ teaspoon kosher salt

1½ teaspoons dried oregano

½ teaspoon freshly ground black pepper

1. Preheat the oven to 425°F. Put the potatoes into a 9-by-13-inch baking dish.

2. In a small bowl, combine the olive oil, chicken or vegetable stock, lemon juice, garlic, salt, oregano, and pepper together and whisk until well mixed. Pour the mixture all over the potatoes, stirring to coat them. Spread the potatoes into a single, even layer in the baking dish.

3. Cover the baking dish tightly with foil. Bake for 20 minutes.

4. Remove the foil, carefully stir and flip the potatoes, then bake for 30 to 40 minutes longer, stirring and flipping carefully once more about halfway through the remaining cooking time. The potatoes should be fork-tender with some golden brown spots here and there. Tip: If crispier potatoes are desired, once the potatoes are done in the oven, cook under the broiler for 3 to 5 minutes (keep a close watch, as they can burn quickly).

MELITZANOSALATA

(EGGPLANT DIP)

YIELD: 4 TO 6 SERVINGS ▪ TIME: 1 HOUR 40 MINUTES ▪ V, V+, GF

Melitzanosalata is one of those dishes you'll likely see on a Greek taverna's meze menu. It's a combination dip/spread, like hummus and tzatziki, except this one's made with roasted eggplants. The old-school way is to fire-roast the eggplants on a grill or other open flame, which gives the dish a little smokiness. Modern recipes, like this one, call for the eggplants to be oven-roasted. To get a similar effect to the traditional version, you can use smoked salt instead of regular kosher salt to add your own smokiness. This recipe is a favorite over at Cabin 11 because it's easy to scale it way up to make a massive batch for sharing with other campers. They add a sprinkling of toasted pine nuts on top, both for a bit of crunch and added texture and flavor and also as a sign of respect to Thalia and her pine tree.

2 eggplants
(about 2 to 3 pounds total)
2 tablespoons pine nuts
2 garlic cloves, grated

Juice of 1 lemon
1 teaspoon kosher salt
¼ cup olive oil,
plus more for serving

2 tablespoons parsley,
finely chopped

1. Heat the oven to 425°F. Line a half-sheet pan with aluminum foil. Pierce the eggplants all over with a sharp knife, then set them on the prepared pan. Roast the eggplants for 45 to 60 minutes, until they are easily pierced with a sharp knife. Set aside until the roasted eggplants are cool enough to safely handle.

2. While the eggplants cool, toast the pine nuts in a dry skillet over medium heat, stirring and tossing frequently, until they are golden in color and have a nutty fragrance, 5 to 8 minutes. Set aside.

3. Once the eggplants have cooled, remove their peels and stems. Place on a clean kitchen towel, gather up the edges of the towel, then twist and squeeze to force out the excess liquid. Alternatively, use a salad spinner to remove the excess liquid if you have one.

4. Place the drained eggplant, garlic, lemon juice, salt, and olive oil in the bowl of a food processor. Pulse until the mixture is smooth, 2 to 4 minutes. Transfer the eggplant dip to a serving bowl, stir in the parsley, then top with a drizzle of olive oil and the toasted pine nuts.

If you don't have a food processor, you can whip the dip vigorously with a fork, but you'll end up with a chunkier final product (though equally delicious!). —Annabeth

HTIPITI
(ROASTED RED PEPPER AND WHIPPED FETA DIP)

YIELD: ABOUT 1 CUP ▪ TIME: 10 MINUTES ▪ V, GF

This star of any meze platter takes the brininess of feta and pairs it with roasted red peppers for a dip that hits all the flavor markers: sweet, salty, sour, a hint of bitterness, and plenty of umami. The best red bell peppers for this dish are ones roasted over the fires of Hades, but if you can't find those, any common grocery store variety will do. I promise you won't be able to taste the difference. This is one of those cases where, yes, you could absolutely roast your own bell peppers without much effort—and you're more than welcome to do so, of course—but you can save yourself a little time by sticking with the store-bought ones. You also have the option to make this dip spicy by using crushed Calabrian chiles—that's totally your call. I hear Clarisse La Rue adds more than one teaspoon of chiles, but she's a competitive one! You can always use less.

8 ounces feta cheese, drained and crumbled

2 roasted red bell peppers from a jar, drained

1 tablespoon red wine vinegar

1 garlic clove, peeled

1 teaspoon Calabrian chile paste (optional)

¼ cup olive oil

1. Place the feta, bell peppers, vinegar, garlic, and chile paste (if using) in the bowl of a food processor. Pulse until combined, about 2 to 3 minutes.

2. With the food processor running, pour in the olive oil in a slow, steady stream until the dip is smooth and creamy. Serve cold with bread or vegetables.

GREEK FRIES

YIELD: SERVES 4 ▪ TIME: 1 HOUR 10 MINUTES ▪ V, GF

Percy claims he simply cannot enjoy a burger without fries. Even Aunty Em served them on the side at her Gnome Emporium. But hers weren't just any old fries. They were Greek style—super crispy, with a little feta, fresh herbs, and a splash of lemon on top—like you might find at a taverna or an American-Greek diner. They're so hard to resist, they can distract even the most resolute hero. They sure did a number on Percy! Of course, if plain fries are more your jam, by all means, swap out the finishing touches for just a little bit of salt. In this case, the word "fries," like the statues in certain gnome emporiums, can be a bit deceptive. These aren't deep-fried at all. Our recipe is all about oven-frying. It takes an extra step or two to make sure your fries turn out nice and crispy, but it's worth the extra effort. You've got this satyr's word on that.

---

2 quarts water

2 tablespoons kosher salt

1 tablespoon vinegar

2 pounds russet potatoes, peeled and cut into ½-inch-by-½-inch-wide batons

¼ cup olive oil

¼ cup feta, drained and crumbled

1 tablespoon fresh oregano leaves, minced

2 tablespoons fresh parsley leaves, minced

2 tablespoons fresh lemon juice

---

1. Place a clean half-sheet pan in the oven, then heat oven to 500°F. Meanwhile, bring the water, salt, and vinegar to a boil in a large pot over high heat. Add the potatoes to your pot, return to a boil, and let cook for 10 minutes, until the potatoes are just tender.

2. Drain the potatoes, then transfer to another clean, half-sheet pan lined with paper towels. Let air dry for 5 to 10 minutes, then transfer to a large bowl. Drizzle with the olive oil, then toss to coat.

3. Carefully place a sheet of parchment on the pan you've preheated in the oven, then dump the fries onto the parchment. Spread into a single layer and bake for 20 minutes.

4. Toss and flip the fries.

5. Reduce the oven temperature to 450°F. Bake for an additional 10 to 15 minutes, until golden and crisp all over.

6. Transfer to a large, heat-proof bowl. While still hot, season to taste with salt, then sprinkle with the feta, oregano, parsley, and lemon juice. Toss to coat, then serve immediately.

ZUCCHINI FRITTERS

YIELD: SERVES 4 ▪ TIME: 10 MINUTES ▪ V

I seem to remember seeing an ad for these zucchini fritters somewhere along our journey. Maybe it was at the sadly defunct Waterland while we were running an errand for Ares. I tried to point them out to Annabeth, but she wouldn't listen. The wispy strands of shredded zucchini are a little too reminiscent of spider legs for some people, I guess. Though whoever heard of a green spider? Wait, don't answer that. I think I hear Annabeth coming. The bottom line is that that these vegetarian fritters are crispy, packed with summery zucchini, fresh herbs, lots of cheese, and a burst of citrus from lemon zest and juice. They're great on their own, but you can always pair them with tzatziki if you're feeling particularly saucy.

2 medium zucchini, ends trimmed

1 teaspoon kosher salt

1 large egg

2 tablespoons fresh dill, minced

1 tablespoon fresh parsley, minced

1 teaspoon lemon zest

4 scallions, white and light-green parts only, thinly sliced

2 garlic cloves, minced

¼ cup feta cheese, drained and crumbled

2 tablespoons grated Parmesan or Pecorino Romano cheese

½ cup all-purpose flour

Olive oil, for frying

Tzatziki (page 72), for serving

1. Shred the zucchini on the largest holes of a box grater. Place the zucchini strands in a clean kitchen towel, gather up the towel sides, and twist and squeeze the fabric to drain out the excess moisture. Transfer the zucchini to a bowl.

2. Season the zucchini with the salt, then add the egg, dill, parsley, lemon zest, scallions, garlic, feta, Parmesan, and flour. Stir to combine all the ingredients.

3. Heat 2 tablespoons of oil in a large skillet over medium heat until it's shimmering. Use a standard ice cream scoop or ¼-cup measure to drop a portion of the fritter mixture onto the skillet. Using the back of a spatula, gently flatten the portion into a ½-inch-thick patty. Repeat this process until you can't fit any more fritters on the pan.

   Don't overcrowd the pan—you should be able to cook 4 to 6 fritters at a time, leaving about an inch between them. —Annabeth

4. Fry the fritters until they are golden brown on the bottom, about 3 to 5 minutes. Flip them, and cook for 3 to 5 minutes longer. If the fritters are browning too quickly, reduce the heat. If the pan looks dry, add more oil as needed. Transfer the cooked fritters to a clean platter.

5. Repeat the cooking process with the remaining fritter mixture until you've used it all up. Serve hot with tzatziki on the side.

CHAPTER FIVE

DINNER: THE FINAL BATTLE

Every day and every quest must come to an end, usually after one last obstacle. If we're speaking in meals, the culmination of the day is, of course, dinner. If it's a quest you're on, there's usually a final battle of some kind. Maybe it's a literal battle, or maybe it's one of those internal struggles where you just have to make a really tough decision. Either way, your journey is coming to a close, which means you'll soon be able to move on to the second-best part of the day (after eating), and that's resting! This chapter is full of end-of-day dishes like Camp Half-Blood BBQ, some classic Greek dinner recipes, and of course, your favorite satyr's favorite dish of all time: bean-and-cheese enchiladas. If you've been cooking your way through this book, you're almost at the finish line!

OVEN BAKED BBQ BRISKET

YIELD: 6 TO 8 SERVINGS · TIME: 5 HOURS · GF

Who would have ever guessed that dryads are natural pit bosses? BBQ pits, that is. Percy looks fondly upon this recipe because brisket was his first dinner when he arrived at Camp Half-Blood. In fact, his new friend Luke was the one who passed the platter to him. You could say that this meal signifies new beginnings. And when we had to go on his quest, it might have been the food Percy most regretted leaving behind, even if he'd had to throw the best, juiciest bite into the fire as an offering to the gods. It's not altogether practical to haul a smoker around when you're on the run from Kindly Ones, but if you have access to a plain old oven, you can still make a great BBQ brisket. The key is to start with a good rub—our recipe below uses an all-purpose version that will suit whichever protein you prefer. It makes about 1 cup of rub, which is more than enough to cover both this brisket and the Oven Baked BBQ Ribs (page 91).

BBQ RUB:

¼ cup dark brown sugar

1 tablespoon smoked salt or kosher salt

2 tablespoons smoked paprika

1 tablespoon onion powder

1 tablespoon ancho chile powder

1 tablespoon dry mustard

1 teaspoon freshly ground black pepper

1 teaspoon garlic powder

1 teaspoon dried oregano

1 teaspoon ground coriander

½ teaspoon ground cumin

BBQ BRISKET:

3- to 4-pound pound brisket, excess fat trimmed

¼ to ⅓ cup BBQ Rub (ingredients above)

1. **TO MAKE THE BBQ RUB:** In a small bowl, combine the brown sugar, salt, paprika, onion powder, ancho chile powder, mustard, pepper, garlic powder, oregano, coriander, and cumin.

2. Whisk together until the ingredients are well-combined.

3. **TO MAKE THE BBQ BRISKET:** Heat the oven to 300°F. Line a half-sheet pan with foil.

4. Lay another sheet of foil on the prepared pan. Place the brisket on top of the foil and rub a generous amount of the BBQ rub (about ¼ to ⅓ cup) all over the surface of the meat. Wrap it tightly with foil, using more foil to completely seal in the brisket if needed—this helps trap moisture in the meat.

5. Transfer the remaining rub to an airtight container and store for up to 1 month at room temperature.

6. Bake the foil-wrapped brisket for 3 to 4 hours, until the meat is easily pierced with a sharp knife. Carefully remove the top layer of foil so that the top of the brisket is exposed.

7. Increase the heat to 400°F and cook the brisket until it is caramelized and well-browned on top, about 25 to 30 minutes longer.

8. Remove the brisket from the oven and let it sit in a warm place for 15 to 20 minutes before carving and serving.

ARES BURGER

YIELD: 4 BURGERS ▪ TIME: 20 MINUTES ▪ V*, V+*

If you've got a fiery spirit (or attitude . . . or temper) like a certain god of war we've run into here and there, you might gravitate toward these burgers. Okay, you don't have to have any kind of fire inside you to enjoy these—you really just have to love spicy foods. That's a prerequisite because these burgers definitely bring the heat. And where there's fire, there's smoke. Wait, I think I have that backward. It's been quite a journey looking out for Percy and Annabeth, okay? Give a satyr a break! The point I'm trying to make here is that these burgers are spicy, both in terms of heat and actual spices. They get some smokiness from cumin and paprika, while Calabrian chiles mixed into the patties themselves and pepper Jack on top combine to bring some sweat-inducing heat. Speaking of sweating, you folks haven't seen Ares around, have you? That guy makes me nervous.

1½ pounds ground beef

1 teaspoon kosher salt

1 teaspoon freshly ground black pepper

½ teaspoon ground cumin

½ teaspoon smoked paprika

2 garlic cloves, finely minced

1 teaspoon crushed Calabrian chile paste

1 tablespoon olive oil

4 slices pepper Jack cheese

4 large hamburger buns or bulkie rolls

4 lettuce leaves

4 tomato slices

4 onion slices

---

1. Crumble the ground beef into a large, wide bowl. Season the meat with the salt, pepper, cumin, paprika, garlic, and Calabrian chile paste. Toss the beef and seasonings together with your hands, taking care not to overwork the meat.

2. Divide the seasoned meat into four 6-ounce patties, gently compressing the meat with your hands. Transfer the patties to a clean plate.

3. Heat the oil in a large skillet over medium-high heat until shimmering. Put the burgers in the skillet and cook, undisturbed, until they are well-browned, 3 to 5 minutes. Flip the burgers and cook them for 3 to 5 minutes longer. Top each patty with a slice of pepper Jack cheese, then cover the skillet for 1 minute to let the cheese melt.

4. Lay the bottom half of a bun or roll on each of four plates. Top each bun bottom with lettuce, then place the burger patties on top of the lettuce. Cover each burger with a slice of tomato and onion, followed by the tops of the buns. Serve immediately.

A plant-based meat substitute could work here, too. Remember to cook according to the package instructions, though. —Annabeth

OVEN BAKED BBQ RIBS

YIELD: SERVES 4 ▪ TIME: 3 HOURS 30 MINUTES ▪ GF

It's hard to say which BBQ item is the favorite at Camp Half-Blood, but ribs rank pretty high up there. Like the BBQ Brisket (page 89), these ribs are prepared in the oven instead of a smoker or grill, but they're still packed with flavor thanks to the BBQ rub used for both recipes. It's versatile and goes nicely with most proteins—fortunately, the recipe makes enough to allow you to experiment. Speaking of experimenting, feel free to play around with different BBQ sauces on this recipe, in addition to the rub, whether you make your own or if you have a favorite store-bought brand. We ran into some pretty good BBQ sauces in St. Louis—sweet and tangy with a spicy, vinegary kick, but use whatever you like. When it comes to food, the only person who can tell you what's good or bad is you!

| ½ cup BBQ Rub (page 89) | 2 racks pork ribs | 2 cups BBQ sauce |

1. Heat the oven to 300°F. Line a half-sheet pan with foil, then lay two additional sheets of foil across the top of the pan.

2. Lay the ribs on the two sheets of foil. Rub each rack of ribs with ¼ cup of the BBQ spice rub, then wrap the racks individually in the sheets of foil. Use more foil if needed to completely seal the ribs.

3. Bake the ribs for 2 to 3 hours, until you can easily pierce the meat between the bones with a sharp knife. Increase the oven temperature to 450°F. Unwrap the ribs, brush both racks with BBQ sauce, and bake for 5 minutes. Brush the ribs with more sauce, then bake for an additional 5 minutes.

4. Let the ribs cool slightly for 10 minutes before slicing and serving with additional BBQ sauce, to taste.

OYAKODON

YIELD: 1 SERVING ▪ TIME: 20 MINUTES

Chiron once mentioned that this classic Japanese dish reminds him of the story of the Cosmic Egg. There are many different versions of this tale all over the world, but I'd guess he was referring to a particular Greek story about how the sky, Uranus, and the earth, Gaia, were originally two halves of an eggshell. Chiron seemed to get a bit lost in thought after that. In English, oyakodon means "parent-and-child bowl," so I can only guess at what was on his mind. But I didn't pry. Eventually, he switched into teacher mode and told me all about this recipe. The preparation is simple: diced chicken and sliced onions gently simmered in a combination of soy sauce, mirin, and sugar. The whole thing is covered with beaten eggs, which slowly cook in the sauce before all is finally placed over the top of steamed rice. There's a special pan you can buy for making this and other donburi (rice bowl dishes), but a small skillet will also do the trick. Speaking of tricks . . . there really isn't one for preparing this recipe. Just don't be tempted to skimp on the cooking time or you may end up with tough pieces of chicken.

OYAKODON SAUCE:

¼ cup warm water

¼ teaspoon instant dashi powder

1 tablespoon soy sauce

1 tablespoon mirin

1 teaspoon brown sugar

OYAKODON:

¼ small onion, thinly sliced

4 to 6 ounces boneless, skinless chicken thighs, cut into 1-inch pieces

2 large eggs, plus 1 egg yolk, beaten

1½ cups cooked short-grain white or brown rice

½ scallion, white and light-green parts only, thinly sliced

1. **TO MAKE THE SAUCE:** Whisk together the water, dashi powder, soy sauce, mirin, and brown sugar in a small bowl until the dashi powder and sugar are dissolved.

2. **TO MAKE THE OYAKODON:** Place the onion slices in the bottom of a cold, 8-inch skillet. Top them with the sauce. Place the skillet over medium heat and bring the sauce to a gentle simmer, lowering the heat if necessary. Cook until the onions soften slightly, 2 to 3 minutes.

3. Carefully add the chicken to the skillet. Heat until the chicken looks almost cooked through with just a hint of pink in the center, about 3 to 4 minutes. Flip the chicken and cook for 2 to 3 minutes longer until fully cooked throughout.

4. Drizzle about ½ the beaten eggs over the center of the chicken. Cover the skillet and let cook until just barely set, 3 to 5 minutes. Uncover, drizzle the remaining egg all over the pan, and replace the cover. Cook until set, about 3 to 5 minutes longer. Remove the pan from the heat.

5. Mound the rice in the center of a deep bowl. Using a wide, slotted spoon or spatula, carefully slide the mass of chicken, egg, and onion out of the pan and onto the top of the rice, leaving most of the sauce in the pan.

6. Drizzle as much of the remaining sauce as you like over the oyakodon, followed by a scattering of sliced scallions. Serve hot.

GROVER'S FAVORITE BEAN-AND-CHEESE ENCHILADAS

YIELD: 4 TO 6 SERVINGS • TIME: 1 HOUR 15 MINUTES • V, GF

At last! I admit that I've been known to lose my beautiful, clever satyr mind over bean-and-cheese enchiladas. They're just a perfect food, as close to ambrosia as I'll ever get to eat. I commend the mortal who invented them. The ones at Yancy Academy were excellent, mostly because I didn't have to make them myself, but also because they were full of rich, flavorful beans, gooey cheese, and covered in a tangy, spicy sauce. When I'm on the go, I'm rarely without my delicious aluminum cans, but if I've got some downtime during a quest, I like to whip these up. Once I'm in the zone with my enchiladas, I feel ready to take on anything: even a Kindly One. But, just to be safe, I still check over my shoulder from time to time . . .

ENCHILADA SAUCE:

3 garlic cloves, peeled

1 small onion, peeled and roughly chopped

4 Roma tomatoes, roughly chopped

3 dried ancho chiles, stemmed and seeded

3 dried guajillo chiles, stemmed and seeded

2 cups vegetable stock

1 teaspoon ground cumin

1 teaspoon freshly ground black pepper

½ teaspoon ground coriander

ENCHILADAS:

2 tablespoons olive oil

1 medium onion, diced

1 red bell pepper, diced

1 medium zucchini, diced

2 garlic cloves, minced

1 teaspoon kosher salt

½ teaspoon freshly ground black pepper

½ teaspoon ground cumin

½ teaspoon ground coriander

¼ teaspoon Mexican oregano

Two 15-ounce cans black beans, drained

6 ounces shredded Colby Jack cheese

Enchilada Sauce (ingredients above)

12 corn tortillas, warmed

1. **TO MAKE THE ENCHILADA SAUCE:** Preheat your oven's broiler and line a half-sheet pan with foil. Lay the garlic, chopped small onion, and tomatoes in a single layer on the pan. Broil the vegetables until they are softened and slightly charred in spots, about 5 to 10 minutes. When you estimate that you have about 1 to 2 minutes left of broiling time, add both the ancho and guajillo chiles to the pan for the remaining time. They should become slightly toasted and pliable.

2. In a medium saucepan over medium-high heat, bring the stock to a simmer. Then, add the garlic, tomatoes, onions, and the chiles from the broiler. Remove the pan from the heat, cover it, and let it sit for 15 minutes, until the chiles are completely rehydrated.

3. Place the contents of the pot, along with the cumin, pepper, and coriander, into a blender and blend until smooth. Pour this sauce through a fine mesh strainer set over a bowl. Discard the solids.

4. **TO MAKE THE ENCHILADAS:** Heat the oil in a large skillet over medium-high heat until shimmering. Add the diced onion, bell pepper, and zucchini. Cook, stirring occasionally, until the vegetables are softened and the onions turn translucent, 7 to 10 minutes.

Broiler strength varies a lot, so keep an eye on your veggies throughout this process. —Annabeth

5. Add the garlic, salt, pepper, cumin, coriander, and oregano. Cook, stirring constantly, until fragrant, about 1 minute longer. Remove the skillet from the heat and stir in the beans, with about ½ of the cheese. This will be the filling.

6. Heat the oven to 400°F. Pour about half the enchilada sauce into the bottom of a 9-by-13-inch baking dish, spreading the sauce into an even layer.

7. Fill each tortilla with about ¼ cup of the bean-and-cheese filling. Roll the tortilla and place it, seam-side down, in the baking dish. Repeat with the remaining tortillas and filling until the baking dish is full.

8. Pour the remaining sauce over the enchiladas and sprinkle the remaining cheese on top. Bake until the enchilada sauce is bubbling and the cheese is melted, 10 to 15 minutes. Let cool slightly before serving.

Moussaka

YIELD: 4 TO 6 SERVINGS • TIME: 2 HOURS

Moussaka is another one of those Greek dishes that has countless variations. Some folks make it with slices of sautéed eggplant, potato, or zucchini, or even a combination of the three. This version includes a blend of mushrooms, which Percy says remind him of the courtyard outside Hades's palace. Not sure why Percy had to bring THAT up during a perfectly pleasant dinner, but here we are. I changed the subject pretty quickly with talk of more idyllic places, and I'd recommend you try to imagine the same. Another word of advice: unless you have several skillets going at once, it can be time-consuming to sauté all of the eggplant you need for a dish like this. To save time, we opt for roasting ours. While the eggplant is in the oven, there's time to prepare the filling so that by the time everything is roasted, you can jump right into assembling your moussaka. I think that kind of speed and efficiency would impress even Hermes himself.

2 small eggplants, cut into ¼-inch-thick rounds

FILLING:

¼ cup olive oil, divided

1 pound ground lamb

8 ounces mixed wild mushrooms, sliced

1 small onion, diced

4 garlic cloves, minced

One 28-ounce can whole peeled plum tomatoes

1½ teaspoons kosher salt

½ teaspoon freshly ground black pepper

2 teaspoons dried oregano

1 teaspoon dried thyme

¼ teaspoon ground cinnamon

Pinch ground clove

Pinch allspice

BÉCHAMEL SAUCE:

¼ cup unsalted butter

¼ cup all-purpose flour

1 cup milk

1 teaspoon kosher salt

½ cup grated Pecorino Romano cheese, divided

2 large eggs, beaten

1. **TO MAKE THE EGGPLANT:** Preheat the oven to 425°F. Line a half-sheet pan with parchment paper. Brush the slices of eggplant with olive oil to coat (it's okay if you don't use all of it). Season with a pinch of salt and pepper, then roast for 20 to 25 minutes until it is golden brown and tender. Set the eggplant aside, then reduce the oven temperature to 400°F.

2. **TO MAKE THE FILLING:** While the eggplant cooks, prepare the filling. Heat 1 tablespoon of olive oil in a large skillet over medium-high heat until shimmering. Add the lamb, mushrooms, and onions. Cook, stirring occasionally and breaking the lamb apart with a wooden spoon, until the meat is well-browned, 10 to 12 minutes. Drain any excess fat from the pan, then return it to the heat.

3. Add the garlic and cook, stirring constantly, for 1 minute.

4. Add the tomatoes, salt, pepper, oregano, thyme, cinnamon, clove, and allspice. Crush the tomatoes with the back of a wooden spoon. Cook, stirring occasionally, until the sauce is reduced and thick, 7 to 10 minutes. Season to taste with additional salt if needed, then remove from the heat.

5. **TO MAKE THE BÉCHAMEL SAUCE:** Melt the butter in a small saucepan over medium heat. Add the flour, whisking constantly, until it starts to smell nutty but doesn't darken, 3 to 5 minutes.

6. Add the milk a little at a time, whisking constantly, until smooth. Let simmer until thickened, about 5 minutes.

7. Whisk in the salt and about half the cheese. Set aside to cool for 10 minutes, then whisk in the eggs.

8. **TO MAKE THE MOUSSAKA:** Lay half the eggplant slices in the bottom of an 8-by-8-inch baking dish, overlapping the slices slightly. Spoon in the filling, lightly compressing it with the back of a spoon. Top with the remaining eggplant slices. Top with the béchamel, followed by the remaining cheese.

9. Bake until golden and bubbling, 20 to 25 minutes. Let cool slightly before slicing and serving.

NYC-STYLE PIZZA

YIELD: 2 PIZZAS • TIME: 2 HOURS 40 MINUTES, PLUS 1 TO 5 DAYS FOR THE DOUGH • V (UNLESS MEAT TOPPINGS ARE USED)

Is there any food more closely associated with New York City than pizza? From the corner joints slinging $2 slices to the sit-down restaurants boasting wood-fired ovens (and deliciously smoky results), pizza is EVERYWHERE in New York. It's almost as ubiquitous as the pigeons, which, on the whole, have a great sense of humor about all the fast-walking pedestrians. Anyway, I've spent enough time in this city with Percy to know that the key to a good New York slice is the dough. For one, you've got to let it ferment in the fridge for a while to develop flavor. This also helps it develop the structure it needs for that famously sturdy crust with just the right amount of chew. Once you get your pizza in the oven, it'll be ready before you can say, EYY! I'M WALKIN' HERE! Just kidding, that would be impossible. But still, it'll be pretty fast.

NYC-STYLE DOUGH:	SAUCE:	PIZZA:
3 cups bread flour	One 28-ounce can peeled plum tomatoes	Pizza Dough (ingredients above)
2 teaspoons kosher salt	2 teaspoons oregano	Cornmeal
2 teaspoons granulated sugar	2 teaspoons kosher salt	Pizza Sauce (ingredients above)
2 teaspoons instant yeast	1½ teaspoons granulated sugar	12 ounces mozzarella cheese, shredded from block
1 cup lukewarm water		Additional toppings as desired, such as pepperoni, mushrooms, diced bell peppers, etc.
3 tablespoons olive oil, plus extra for greasing your container		

1. **TO MAKE THE NYC-STYLE DOUGH:** Combine the flour, salt, and sugar in the bowl of a food processor. Pulse to mix the ingredients well (don't skip this—it'll help prevent the salt and yeast from coming into contact with each other later, which can harm the yeast).

2. Add the yeast, water, and olive oil to the food processor. Pulse to combine, then process continuously until a smooth, elastic dough forms, about 2 to 3 minutes.

3. Brush the inside of a large bowl or 4-quart sealable storage container with a little extra olive oil, then set the dough inside it. Cover the bowl or seal the container, and let the dough rise in the refrigerator for at least 24 hours, or up to 5 days.

4. **TO MAKE THE SAUCE:** Add the tomatoes, oregano, 2 teaspoons of salt, and 1½ teaspoons of sugar into the bowl of a food processor. Pulse until the mixture is mostly smooth with some very small chunks of tomato (lentil-size chunks at the largest) remaining. Transfer the sauce to an airtight container and store in the refrigerator until you're ready to use it. Sauce may be prepared up to 5 days in advance.

5. **TO MAKE THE PIZZA:** Remove the dough from the fridge about 2 hours before you plan to make pizza and allow it to come to room temperature. Place a pizza stone on the middle rack of your oven, then heat the oven to 500°F. If you don't have a pizza stone, just invert a half-sheet pan and preheat that instead.

6. Dust a pizza peel liberally with cornmeal—if you don't have a pizza peel, dust another inverted half-sheet pan with cornmeal. Divide the dough into two equal portions. Stretch one portion out to make a 14-inch round. Transfer the round to the pizza peel or inverted pan. Then, working quickly, top the dough with about ½ cup of the sauce, 6 ounces (about half) of the cheese, and your desired toppings. Stick to a maximum of about 1 cup of additional toppings besides the cheese.

7. Using the pizza peel or inverted pan, slide the pizza onto the preheated stone or other inverted pan in the oven. Bake until the crust is golden and the cheese is melted with some golden spots, 7 to 10 minutes. Repeat the process with the remaining dough. Slice and serve while pizzas are still hot.

AVGoLEMoNo

YIELD: 4 TO 6 SERVINGS ▪ TIME: 1 HOUR 30 MINUTES ▪ GF

This classic soup is a favorite of the campers in Cabin 7—they say the warm, lemony flavor reminds them of sunshine. This dish's name quite literally means EGG LEMON, which is, well, really on-the-nose, because those are two of the main ingredients. Keep it simple, I guess. While the lemon juice adds flavor and acidity, the eggs add richness and body, actually thickening the soup to more of a stew-like consistency. Since the name really only applies to the broth, you can customize this to your hearts' delight with various proteins or vegetables. You can even switch out the rice for a different grain or maybe use traditional orzo (just adjust the cooking times as needed using the package instructions). This version just includes chicken and rice, but you could easily add some diced carrots, celery, or other vegetables to the mix when you simmer the chicken.

2 bone-in, skin-on chicken breasts (2 to 3 pounds total)

2 quarts low-sodium chicken stock

1 cup arborio rice

3 large eggs

½ cup lemon juice

2 tablespoons fresh dill leaves, minced, plus more for serving

1. Place the chicken breasts in a medium saucepan. Pour in the chicken stock, then place the pan over medium-high heat. Bring the stock to a boil, then reduce the heat and simmer, uncovered, until the chicken is cooked through, 30 to 35 minutes, or until an instant-read thermometer registers 150°F when inserted into the thickest part of the chicken. As the chicken cooks, be sure to skim off any foam that rises to the top of the pot. Transfer the chicken to a clean plate to cool, reserving the stock.

2. Return the stock to a boil, then add the arborio rice. Reduce the heat to a simmer and cook until the rice is tender, 20 to 25 minutes. Reduce the heat again, until the soup is barely simmering.

3. In a medium, heat-proof bowl, beat the eggs and lemon juice together until smooth. While whisking constantly, use a ladle to slowly pour some of the chicken stock into the egg mixture. Repeat until you've transferred about ⅓ of the stock to the egg mixture. Then, stirring constantly, pour the contents of the bowl into the original saucepan.

4. Shred the chicken and return it to the saucepan, discarding the skin and bones. Cook the soup, stirring and scraping the sides constantly, until thickened, about 5 to 10 minutes longer.

5. Remove the pan from the heat, then stir in the fresh dill. Ladle the soup into bowls, garnish with more fresh dill, and serve.

SISYPHEAN MEATBALL ON A HILL OF SPAGHETTI

YIELD: 8 SERVINGS · TIME: 1 HOUR

Spaghetti and meatballs is a classic Italian-American dish beloved by mortals both young and . . . well, in the scheme of things, I wouldn't call mortals OLD, but maybe FULL-GROWN would apply? Usually you see a plate of marinara-laden spaghetti with a few small meatballs here and there, but this version opts for one giant meatball instead. I remember the first time I saw it, at an Italian restaurant in New York City with Percy. There it was, a hill of spaghetti with an epic meatball sitting precariously on top. I knew I'd seen something like it before, and then it struck me: Sisyphus and his boulder. When the waiter stood there grating a mound of fluffy white Parmesan over the top, I swear I could hear Sisyphus groaning in the distance as if to say, AW, COME ON! In this recipe, we roast the meatballs in the oven to get them brown and crispy on the outside, then simmer them in homemade tomato sauce—the meatballs impart their flavor to the sauce and vice versa.

MEATBALLS:
1 pound ground beef

1 pound ground pork

1 cup ricotta

½ cup grated Parmesan

2 large eggs

¾ cup breadcrumbs

1 tablespoon fresh oregano, minced

1 tablespoon fresh parsley, minced

5 garlic cloves, minced

2 teaspoons kosher salt

1 teaspoon freshly ground black pepper

SPAGHETTI:
¼ cup olive oil

8 garlic cloves, minced

Pinch red pepper flakes

Two 28-ounce cans whole peeled plum tomatoes

2 teaspoons kosher salt

1 teaspoon freshly ground black pepper

1 teaspoon dried oregano

2 basil sprigs

1 pound dried spaghetti

Grated Parmesan, for serving

1. **TO MAKE THE MEATBALLS:** Heat the oven to 400°F. Line a half-sheet pan with parchment paper.

2. Crumble the ground beef and pork into a large mixing bowl. Add the ricotta, ½ cup of Parmesan, eggs, breadcrumbs, 1 tablespoon each of the oregano and parsley, 5 cloves of minced garlic, 2 teaspoons of salt, and 1 teaspoon of pepper. Using your hands, gently mix the ingredients until they are well distributed.

3. Shape the meat mixture into eight large balls, then transfer them to the prepared pan. Roast the meatballs until they are deeply browned all over, 25 to 35 minutes.

4. **TO MAKE THE SPAGHETTI:** Heat the oil in a large Dutch oven over medium heat, then add 8 cloves of minced garlic. Cook, stirring constantly, until fragrant and lightly browned, 2 to 3 minutes. Add the tomatoes, 2 teaspoons of salt, 1 teaspoon each of pepper and oregano, and basil. Increase the heat and bring the sauce to a boil while mashing the tomatoes with a potato masher or the back of a wooden spoon.

5. Let the sauce simmer until the meatballs are done baking, remove the basil sprigs from the sauce, then add the meatballs to the sauce. Cover the pot and continue simmering the sauce with the meatballs, stirring occasionally, until the sauce is reduced and thickened, about 15 to 20 minutes longer. Transfer the meatballs to a serving platter.

6. Bring a large pot of salted water to a boil over high heat. Cook the pasta to al dente according to the package instructions.

7. Transfer the cooked pasta to the pot of tomato sauce, along with about ½ cup of the pasta water. Gently stir to coat the pasta in the sauce.

8. Use a pair of tongs or a pasta fork to twist up a serving of pasta. Carefully transfer it to a shallow bowl, holding the tongs upright and then slowly releasing the pasta so it sits in a large mound. Top each serving with a meatball, followed by grated Parmesan, and serve.

ST. LOUIS-STYLE PIZZA

YIELD: 2 PIZZAS ▪ TIME: 45 MINUTES ▪ V (UNLESS USING MEAT TOPPINGS)

If you're not from St. Louis, you may not realize that it has its very own style of pizza. Percy, Annabeth, and I had never heard of it until our quest took us through the city, but it's a fascinating piece of American food history. For one, the crust is super thin, almost like a gigantic cracker. And it's not a yeast-based crust, which is nice because that means you can make a St. Louis-style pizza faster than any other kind. The other big difference is the cheese. They use a special processed cheese called Provel, which is like a mix of provolone, cheddar, and Swiss with smoky flavor added. Provel can be tricky to find outside of Missouri, but you can try a blend of shredded cheddar, mozzarella or provolone, and smoked Gouda instead and get a pizza that's pretty close to the real thing. The sauce itself is traditional, so feel free to follow the recipe from the New York slice on page 98, or opt for a store-bought version.

ST. LOUIS-STYLE DOUGH:
2 cups all-purpose flour
2 teaspoons baking powder
1 teaspoon kosher salt
2 tablespoons olive oil
½ cup warm water

PIZZA:
St. Louis-Style Dough
(ingredients above)
1 cup pizza sauce (page 98)

12 ounces shredded Provel, or a blend of shredded white cheddar, mozzarella or provolone, and smoked Gouda
Additional toppings as desired, such as pepperoni, mushrooms, diced bell peppers, etc.

1. Preheat the oven to 450°F.

2. **TO MAKE THE ST. LOUIS-STYLE DOUGH:** In a large bowl, whisk together the flour, baking powder, and salt. Stir in the olive oil and warm water, mixing until a stiff dough forms. Divide the dough into two equal-size balls, then roll out to large, thin rounds.

3. Sandwich one of the rounds between two sheets of parchment paper. Roll the dough to a thickness of about ⅛ inch. The round should be roughly 12 inches across. Peel off the top layer of parchment paper, then transfer the crust, still on the bottom layer of parchment paper, to a half-sheet pan. Repeat with the remaining dough round.

4. **TO MAKE THE PIZZA:** Spread ½ cup of pizza sauce on each crust, sprinkle about 6 ounces of cheese on each, then add your preferred toppings. If you are using a blend of cheeses, toss them together in a large bowl until they are well mixed before sprinkling on the pizzas.

5. Bake the pizzas for 10 to 12 minutes, until the crusts are lightly golden and the cheese has melted. Rotate the pizzas about halfway through the baking time to ensure even browning.

CHAPTER SIX

DESSERT: THE SWEET TASTE OF VICTORY

Whether you've been on a world-altering quest or you've just had a long day, you survived! As far as I'm concerned, there's nothing left for you to do but savor the sweet taste of victory.

And I mean that literally. My personal post-quest ritual starts with a sweet treat before a long rest. I've included a whole range of dessert options so you can celebrate according to your own tastebuds. Maybe you want some honey-sweetened cheesecake, or Percy's Blue Velvet Cake, or some of Sally Jackson's Blue Chocolate Chip Cookies. If you're not feeling up to a big project, you could whip up a tasty trio of milkshakes or a classic New York Egg Cream. Percy would probably say that you don't have to wait until the end of the day for something sweet. Of course, he'd also know that once a big quest is over, another might just be beginning . . . Either way, this chapter has got you covered.

FRIED PEARLS
(LOUKOUMADES)

YIELD: 8 TO 12 SERVINGS · TIME: 2 HOURS 20 MINUTES · V

Loukoumades are tiny Greek donuts, bite-size, glorious, and covered in sticky, sweet honey. They're small and round, like little golden pearls, but with a crisp exterior and fluffy interior. By adding black luster dust (that's edible pigment powder that can give food and beverages a blast of color with a metallic sheen) to the honey, you can make your loukoumades look an awful lot like the pearls that Percy, Annabeth, and I used to escape Hades's domain. The black luster dust makes the honey all shiny and pearlescent, almost as mesmerizing as it is delicious. Of course, your loukoumades won't have any actual magical properties, though you might find that they have a way of magically disappearing every time you make them.

LOUKOUMADES DOUGH:
1 cup milk, warmed
3 tablespoons sugar
1 teaspoon active dry yeast

3 cups flour
1 teaspoon kosher salt
2 quarts vegetable oil, for frying

HONEY SAUCE:
½ cup honey
2 teaspoons lemon juice
½ teaspoon black luster dust

1. **TO MAKE THE DOUGH:** Whisk the milk and sugar together in a small bowl until the sugar dissolves. Stir in the yeast and let the mixture sit for 5 to 10 minutes, until foamy.

2. Put the flour and salt into the bowl of a food processor and pulse to combine. Then, with the food processor running continuously, pour in the yeast mixture and process until a soft, slightly sticky dough forms, about 2 to 3 minutes.

3. Transfer the dough to a large, lightly oiled bowl. Cover the bowl and let the dough rise for 60 to 90 minutes, until it has doubled in volume.

4. **TO MAKE THE HONEY SAUCE:** Heat the honey in a small saucepan over low heat until it becomes runny. Stir in the lemon juice and black luster dust. Remove the pan from the heat and let the sauce cool to room temperature.

5. **TO MAKE THE LOUKOUMADES:** Heat the oil in a large Dutch oven to 350°F. Line a half-sheet pan with paper towels and set a wire cooling rack inside the pan, over the towels.

6. Gently punch the risen dough back down in the bowl. Then, lightly oil your hands and a 1-tablespoon measuring spoon.

7. Grip some of the dough in your oil-coated hand, squeezing gently so that the dough is pushed out through the space between your thumb and forefinger—this will pull the dough taut, while also helping you portion it out. Use the measuring spoon to scoop off a rounded tablespoon-size piece of dough. Repeat this process until you have used all of the dough to create equal-size balls.

8. Working in batches, fry the dough balls, stirring and flipping them occasionally, until they are uniformly golden all over, about 6 to 8 minutes. Transfer the donuts to the prepared wire rack to drain.

9. Repeat the process until all of the dough balls are fried. Pile the donuts on a serving platter. Stir the honey sauce to reincorporate any ingredients that may have separated, then drizzle the sauce all over the donuts. Serve warm.

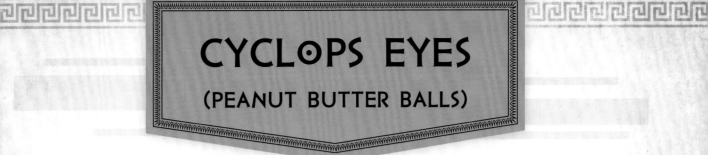

CYCLOPS EYES
(PEANUT BUTTER BALLS)

YIELD: ABOUT 2 DOZEN • TIME: 1 HOUR • V, GF

When Percy was much younger, he used to notice all sorts of strange things, like a tall man in a trench coat keeping his one eye trained on him. I bet that would have been hard for Sally Jackson to explain to her son. From what I know about Percy and how he and his fellow half-bloods draw . . . attention, my guess is that he came face-to-face with a Cyclops. But who can be sure? This sweet treat is much less ambiguous, though after you whip up a batch, it may give you the sneaking suspicion that you're being watched. Unlike an actual group of Cyclopes, these confections are both sweet and salty, always a winning combo. Many Cyclopes are just, well, salty. On the other hand, I know one who is sweet as can be.

½ cup unsalted butter, room temperature

1 cup creamy peanut butter

1½ teaspoons vanilla extract

2½ cups powdered sugar

6 ounces dark chocolate, chopped

1½ teaspoons coconut oil

Refined coconut oil will not change the taste of the chocolate. However, virgin coconut oil will add a coconut flavor—use whichever you prefer. —Annabeth

You can do this by hand, too, but prepared to put some work into it. —Annabeth

1. In a large bowl, combine the butter, peanut butter, and vanilla extract, using a handheld electric mixer on medium speed to beat the ingredients until they create a smooth and creamy mixture, about 2 to 4 minutes. Add the powdered sugar and beat at low speed until the mixture turns to a soft, pliable dough.

2. Line a half-sheet pan with parchment paper. Using a measuring spoon or cookie scoop, measure out 1-tablespoon portions of peanut butter mixture. Roll the portions into individual balls and place them on the prepared pan.

3. Freeze the peanut butter balls for 15 to 20 minutes, until they are firm and very cold.

4. While the peanut butter balls are in the freezer, combine the chocolate and coconut oil in a small, heat-proof bowl. Set the bowl over a small saucepan of barely simmering water. Gently heat the chocolate and oil, stirring constantly, until the mixture is melted and smooth. Let this chocolate coating cool slightly.

5. Remove the peanut butter balls from the freezer. Working one at a time, use a toothpick to pierce the peanut butter balls and carefully dip them in the chocolate, leaving a small circle of peanut butter exposed on each "eye" and allowing the excess to back into the bowl. Place the dipped candies back on the parchment paper.

6. The chocolate should harden fairly quickly. Before it does, use the back of a spoon or an offset spatula to smooth over the holes created by the toothpicks. Then, allow the candies to set completely.

7. Serve the Cyclops Eyes cold or at room temperature. Store any leftovers in an airtight container in the refrigerator for up to 1 week.

CERBERUS'S PET-FRIENDLY TREATS

YIELD: VARIES, DEPENDING ON COOKIE-CUTTER-SIZE ▪ TIME: 40 MINUTES ▪ V

Thanks to Annabeth's quick thinking in the Underworld, we know that Cerberus is actually a very good boy (or wait, is he three good boys?) who just wants to play. The big ol' cuddle monster loves red rubber balls especially. While none of us has any real driving desire to go back across the river Styx, I think I speak for all when I say we don't feel the same dread about seeing that big pup again. And if there's a next time, we won't go empty-handed because every good dog deserves treats, Cerberus triply so. We'd go the extra mile to show just how much we love him by making him this pup-friendly recipe ourselves. Oh, and humans can eat them, too—just don't expect them to be terribly sweet. Annabeth researched the ingredients to make sure they're safe for both dogs and people. If you've got a good little pupperino in your life that you want to share a treat with, we've got a vet-approved recipe ready to go. Still, it's always best to double check with your own vet to make sure these ingredients are okay for your particular dog's diet.

Use cookie cutters that are appropriately sized for your dog. Additionally, you can choose to bake soft treats, or harder crunchier versions depending on your dog's needs. Simply adjust the bake time as needed. Ginger is typically safe for most dogs, but it may not be suitable for dogs with certain conditions. Check with your vet to make sure ginger is okay, or omit it entirely if you're unsure. —Annabeth

---

½ cup pumpkin puree

1 small banana, mashed (about ½ cup)

1 large egg

1 cup creamy peanut butter

¾ teaspoon ground ginger (optional)

2¼ cups whole wheat flour

---

1. Preheat the oven to 350°F. Line a half-sheet pan with parchment paper.

2. In a large mixing bowl, beat together the pumpkin, banana, egg, peanut butter, and ginger (if using) with a handheld electric mixer until smooth. Mix in the wheat flour until a smooth dough forms.

   You can also do this by hand, with a wooden spoon. —Annabeth

3. Roll the dough out on a liberally floured work surface to a thickness of about ½ inch. Use a cookie cutter, preferably bone-shaped, to stamp out as many treats as you can. Transfer the treats to the prepared pan, leaving about ½ inch between them. They won't spread much at all, so you can keep them fairly close together. Gather up and combine any scraps of dough to roll out again. Then stamp more treats until you have enough to fill the pan.

4. Bake for 15 to 20 minutes, depending on how crunchy you want them to be. If you have dough left, repeat the process until you've used it all up. Store the treats in an airtight container at room temperature for up to 1 week.

BAKLAVA

YIELD: ABOUT 3 DOZEN · TIME: 2 HOURS · V

This golden, flaky sweet is soaked in a syrup made with honey, which some have called the nectar of the gods. Though if anything I've heard about that sort of nectar is true, it tastes different for everyone who eats it. That's the case with baklava, too, as there are many ways to approach it. I like a combination of pistachios and almonds, but you can make it with any of your favorite nuts—just substitute walnuts, pecans, or hazelnuts for some or all of the nuts in this recipe. Many of the campers at Camp Half-Blood love this baklava so much that they claim it's what ambrosia tastes like. I'll have to take their word for it, since I'm not a demigod. I'm more than happy to just enjoy baklava for its own sake, though. It may not have restorative powers like ambrosia, but hey, I'm not greedy. I will, however, eat a whole pan of baklava if left to my own devices.

Follow the package instructions for thawing your phyllo pastry. Typically, you can thaw it in the refrigerator for a few hours, or at room temperature for an hour or so. The refrigerator method is a little more foolproof, especially if your kitchen runs warm. Phyllo usually comes in two packs in a single 1-pound package. As you work through the recipe, it's best to start with one package, keeping the other in the refrigerator while you work. —Annabeth

HONEY SYRUP:
1 cup honey
1 cup granulated sugar
1 cup water
2 teaspoons orange zest
½ teaspoon orange blossom water

BAKLAVA FILLING:
2 cups raw, shelled pistachios
1½ cups raw, shelled almonds
½ cup dark brown sugar
1 tablespoon ground cinnamon

One 1-pound package phyllo dough, thawed
¾ cup unsalted butter, melted

1. **TO MAKE THE HONEY SYRUP:** In a small saucepan over medium-high heat, bring the honey, cup of sugar, water, and orange zest to a boil. Stirring constantly, continue to boil the mixture until it is reduced and slightly thickened, about 10 minutes.

2. Remove the pan from the heat and stir in the orange blossom water. Set the syrup aside in a warm place.

3. **TO MAKE THE BAKLAVA:** Add the pistachios, almonds, brown sugar, and cinnamon to the bowl of a food processor. Pulse until finely ground, 3 to 5 minutes. Set the nut mixture aside.

4. Preheat the oven to 400°F. Brush the bottom and sides of a 9-by-13-inch baking dish with some of the melted butter.

5. Open one pack of the phyllo dough, if your package is divided into two packs. Otherwise, separate out ½ pound of dough. Unroll it onto a clean work surface. Check the size of the phyllo—if it's 9 by 13 inches, leave it alone. Otherwise, trim the stack of phyllo sheets with a very sharp knife, using your baking dish as a guide. Soak a clean kitchen towel or paper towel in water, then squeeze most of the water out, leaving the towel damp. Gently lay the damp towel on top of the phyllo while you work to keep it from drying out.

6. Lay one sheet of phyllo in the buttered baking dish. Brush the sheet liberally with butter, then lay another sheet of phyllo on top of the first. Repeat until you've used up the whole package of phyllo.

7. Tip the nut filling into the baking dish, spreading it across the whole pan and gently compressing it with your hands.

8. Open the second package of phyllo or gather your remaining ½ pound of phyllo. Lay it out on the work surface and cover it with the damp towel (re-wet and wring out the towel if it has dried out). Lay a sheet of phyllo on the nut filling. Brush with butter, then lay another sheet of phyllo on top. Repeat until all of the phyllo and butter has been used, making sure to butter the top layer.

9. Wet a very sharp knife. Slice the baklava along the length of the pan using a short sawing motion to make rows about 1 to 1½ inches wide. Make sure you cut all the way to the bottom of the pan, through every layer of phyllo. Wet the knife as often as needed to keep the pastry and filling from sticking to it. Make similar cuts at an angle across the pan to create diamond shapes or make cuts along the width of the pan if you prefer your baklava in squares or rectangles.

10. Bake the baklava for 50 to 75 minutes, until it is deeply golden brown and flaky. Start checking for doneness every 5 minutes starting at the 50-minute mark.

11. Once the baklava is done baking, remove it from the oven and slowly pour the honey syrup all over the top and down the sides and edges. Set the baking dish on a wire cooling rack and let the baklava cool to room temperature before serving.

BLUE VELVET CAKE

YIELD: 8 TO 12 SERVINGS • TIME: 1 HOUR 30 MINUTES, PLUS COOLING TIME • V

There's not a person in this life or the afterlife who Sally Jackson loves more than her son Percy. She's gone to great lengths to protect him and ensure that he had a normal childhood for as long as possible. When he latched onto blue foods as a kid, wouldn't you know it, a big blue cake showed up for his next birthday. And every birthday after that. The recipe is not unlike that of a classic red velvet cake, a southern United States specialty that found its way to New York and even became a signature dessert at a popular Manhattan hotel. The main difference is that Sally uses food coloring to turn it a deep ocean blue. Of course, the cream cheese frosting on the outside is also dyed blue because consistency matters, people.

BATTER:
2½ cups cake flour, divided
1 teaspoon baking soda
1¼ teaspoons kosher salt
1½ cups sugar
1 cup neutral oil
½ cup butter, softened
3 large eggs, room temperature

1 tablespoon vanilla extract
1 ounce blue
liquid food coloring
1 tablespoon distilled
white vinegar
1 cup buttermilk, room
temperature, divided

FROSTING:
½ cup unsalted butter, room
temperature
1 pound cream cheese, room
temperature
1 pound powdered sugar
2 teaspoons vanilla extract
4 drops sky blue gel food
coloring

1. Heat the oven to 350°F. Grease three 8-inch round cake pans, and line the bottoms with parchment rounds.

2. **TO MAKE THE BATTER:** In a small bowl, whisk together the flour, baking soda, and salt.

3. In the bowl of a stand mixer fitted with a paddle attachment, beat together the sugar, oil, and butter on medium speed until the mixture is smooth. With the mixer running, add the eggs one at a time, allowing each to be fully incorporated before adding the next one. Mix in 1 tablespoon of vanilla extract, 1 ounce of food coloring, and the distilled white vinegar.

4. Reduce the mixer speed to low. Add ⅓ of the flour mixture and mix until it is incorporated. Add ½ cup of the buttermilk and let mix until smooth. Mix in another ⅓ of the flour mixture until smooth. Mix in the remaining ½ cup of buttermilk until smooth, then stop the mixer and scrape batter from the paddle and down the sides and bottom of the bowl. Beat in the remaining ⅓ flour mixture until the batter is smooth.

   You can also use a handheld electric mixer or do this by hand.
   —Annabeth

5. Divide the batter evenly among the prepared cake pans. Bake for 20 to 25 minutes, until a cake tester or toothpick comes out mostly clean with a few moist crumbs clinging to it when inserted into the center of the cakes. Let the 3 cake layers cool in their respective pans for about 10 minutes before carefully transferring them to a wire rack to cool completely.

6. **TO MAKE THE FROSTING:** In a large bowl, beat the butter and cream cheese together with a handheld electric mixer on high speed until the mixture is light and fluffy, 5 to 7 minutes. Reduce the mixer speed to low and mix in the pound of powdered sugar until it is just moistened, then increase the speed to high and mix until smooth, 5 to 7 minutes. Beat in 2 teaspoons of vanilla extract, followed by 4 drops of blue food coloring gel.

7. If the cake layers have domed, trim their tops with a long, serrated knife so that they're flat and level. Place one cake layer on a platter or cake stand. Top it with a heaping ½ cup of frosting, spreading it out in an even layer with an offset spatula. Repeat with the second layer of cake and another ½ cup of frosting. Top the cake with the third layer and spread the remaining frosting over the top and sides of the whole cake. Slice and serve.

BLUE CHOCOLATE CHIP COOKIES

YIELD: ABOUT 2½ DOZEN COOKIES • TIME: 1 HOUR • V

Like Picasso, Percy has had a blue period. Unlike Picasso, though, Percy's never left his and, honestly, probably never will. Why should he? It's working out for him so far, right? Minus the y'know, constant run-ins with Kindly Ones, angry gods on the brink of war, trips to the Underworld, Lotus Eaters . . . hmmm. Y'know, Percy really hasn't had the best luck after all, has he? That guy deserves a cookie. Just a nice little treat to comfort him and remind him of home. Fortunately, we've got Sally Jackson's recipe for electric blue chocolate chip cookies. Percy says they always hit the spot, especially when they're fresh from the oven. But is there really such a thing as a bad chocolate chip cookie? Maybe one made by someone from Cabin 5, but that's just because they'd probably do it on purpose as part of some prank.

2½ cups all-purpose flour

1½ teaspoons kosher salt

¾ teaspoon baking soda

¾ teaspoon baking powder

1½ cups light brown sugar, lightly packed

½ cup granulated sugar

1 cup butter, softened

1 tablespoon vanilla extract

4 to 6 drops electric blue gel food coloring

1 large egg

12 ounces dark chocolate chips

---

1. Heat the oven to 350°F. Line a half-sheet pan with parchment paper.

2. In a medium-size bowl, whisk together the flour, salt, baking soda, and baking powder. Set flour mixture aside.

3. In the bowl of a stand mixer fitted with a paddle attachment, cream together the brown sugar, granulated sugar, butter, and vanilla extract until the mixture is light and fluffy, 3 to 5 minutes.

4. Beat the gel food coloring into the sugar-and-butter mixture, followed by the egg.

5. Reduce the mixer speed to low, then add in the bowl of flour mixture and mix until incorporated. Mix in the chocolate chips.

6. Use a 2-tablespoon cookie scoop or spoon to portion out the dough. Place the portions of dough on the prepared half-sheet pan, spacing them about 2 inches apart. Keep in mind that you will have dough leftover.

7. Bake for 11 to 13 minutes until the cookies are just golden on the edges and set in the middle.

8. Let the cookies cool on the pan for 5 minutes, then transfer them to a wire cooling rack to cool completely. Store cookies in an airtight container for up to 1 week.

9. Repeat steps 6, 7, and 8 with the remaining dough.

You can also keep the portioned dough in a resealable storage bag in the freezer for up to 2 months. You can bake cookies from frozen—just add a couple of minutes to the bake time. —Annabeth

VANILLA, CHOCOLATE, OR STRAWBERRY MILKSHAKES

YIELD: 2 MILKSHAKES ▪ TIME: 10 MINUTES ▪ V, GF

Percy tells me that a meal consisting of a burger and fries is simply not complete without a milkshake. And who am I to argue? We certainly had our share of milkshakes throughout our journey across America to stop the war between the gods (and I'd say we earned them). Milkshakes are a mainstay at diners and ice cream parlors all across this country, but you don't have to leave your house to get some of that cold, rich, creamy goodness in a glass. It doesn't take a ton of ingredients, whether you're making the vanilla, chocolate, or strawberry version of this recipe. There's certainly something magical about that last one that I can't quite put my finger on. No matter your milkshake of choice, the steps are pretty much the same. You may be tempted to use chocolate ice cream for a chocolate milkshake, but many of our favorite establishments used flavored syrups with vanilla ice cream. According to one kind and patient server, you'd risk diluting the chocolate ice cream with the milk and may end up with something not as optimally chocolaty.

VANILLA MILKSHAKE:
1 pint vanilla ice cream

2 tablespoons malted milk powder

1 teaspoon vanilla extract or paste

½ cup ice-cold milk

Whipped cream

Rainbow sprinkles

Maraschino cherry

CHOCOLATE MILKSHAKE:
1 pint vanilla ice cream

2 tablespoons malted milk powder

4 tablespoons chocolate syrup

½ cup ice-cold milk

Whipped cream

Chocolate sprinkles

Maraschino cherry

STRAWBERRY MILKSHAKE:
1 pint vanilla ice cream

2 tablespoons malted milk powder

4 tablespoons strawberry syrup

½ cup ice-cold milk

Whipped cream

2 strawberries, diced

1. Let the ice cream sit out at room temperature for about 5 minutes to soften slightly. Meanwhile, place the malted milk powder and either the vanilla extract, chocolate syrup, or strawberry syrup in a blender.

2. Using a spoon or ice cream scoop, break apart and scoop the ice cream into the blender. Pour in the milk and blend until smooth, about 1 to 2 minutes.

3. Divide the milkshake between two glasses. For the vanilla or chocolate milkshakes, top with whipped cream, sprinkles, and a cherry. For the strawberry milkshake, replace the sprinkles and cherry with diced strawberries.

NECTAR: CHOCOLATE CHIP COOKIE SMOOTHIE

YIELD: 2 SMOOTHIES ▪ TIME: 10 MINUTES ▪ V

Sometimes I get a little jealous that demigods get to drink nectar. The first time Percy ever tried it himself, he mentioned that it tasted just like his mom's chocolate chip cookies, but in milkshake form. While I can't actually have it myself, I can have the next best thing by making a milkshake using Sally Jackson's Blue Chocolate Chip Cookies (page 117). Now, you don't HAVE to make chocolate chip cookies from scratch for this recipe to work, especially if you've already got some store-bought chocolate chip cookies kicking around in your pantry. (That couldn't be me—they'd never last that long.) If you DO opt for store-bought cookies, you can tailor the final product to your taste by getting your favorite kind, especially if they're baked fresh at a bakery! Just remember to leave at least one extra to crumble on top for garnish. We use frozen yogurt here instead of ice cream to tame a bit of the sweetness from the cookies. So I'm calling it a smoothie. I don't think Percy will mind, though.

1 pint vanilla frozen yogurt	3 to 4 Blue Chocolate Chip Cookies (page 117), plus more for garnishing	1 cup ice-cold milk

1. Let the frozen yogurt sit out at room temperature for 5 minutes to soften slightly.

2. Crumble the cookies into a blender, reserving a handful of cookie crumbs to use as garnish—about 1 or 2 tablespoons of crumbs per smoothie is plenty.

3. Use a spoon or ice cream scoop to break apart the frozen yogurt and scoop it into the blender. Pour the milk over the top, then blend until smooth, about 1 to 2 minutes.

4. Divide the smoothie between two glasses and top with crumbled cookies. Serve with straws and spoons.

AMBROSIA: POPCORN-INFUSED PUDDING

YIELD: ABOUT 4 CUPS • TIME: 30 MINUTES, PLUS 4 HOURS TO CHILL • V, GF

Ambrosia is another special food that, like nectar, can heal wounds. It's also what gives gods their immortality! Of course, if a demigod has too much of it, there are some pretty gnarly consequences. Ever have heartburn? Think that, but a lot more literal. Fortunately, the only thing you have to worry about with this dessert is getting a bit of a tummy ache if you eat too much of it. One of the coolest things about ambrosia is that it tastes different for everyone. The first time Annabeth had it, she noticed it tasted like buttered popcorn, which says a lot about her. Specifically, it says that one of her favorite foods is buttered popcorn! Alright, so that's not a lot, per se, but you can tell a lot about someone based on what their favorite foods are. Like how bean-and-cheese enchilada fans are destined for great things . . .

2 cups milk	¾ cup sugar	3 tablespoons cornstarch
1 cup half-and-half	¼ teaspoon kosher salt	5 large egg yolks
3 cups popped, buttered popcorn	Pinch nutmeg	2 tablespoons unsalted butter

1. Bring the milk and half-and-half to a simmer in a medium saucepan or saucier over medium heat. Stir in the popcorn, then remove the pan from the heat. Cover the pan and let steep for 20 minutes.

2. Pour the infused milk through a strainer set over a bowl. Press down on the solid popcorn pieces to push out all of the flavorful milk mixture. Discard the solids.

3. In a separate bowl, whisk together the sugar, salt, nutmeg, and cornstarch, breaking up any clumps. Then, whisk in the egg yolks until smooth. Add the infused milk mixture and whisk to combine, creating your pudding base.

4. Transfer the pudding base to the saucepan. Bring the mixture to a gentle simmer, whisking constantly, over medium heat. When the mixture begins to bubble, start a 1-minute timer and continue whisking constantly. Remove the pan from the heat when the timer goes off.

5. Strain the pudding into a bowl, discarding any remaining solids. Then whisk in the butter.

6. Press a piece of plastic wrap onto the surface of the pudding and chill it in the fridge for at least 4 hours before serving.

S'MORES

YIELD: ABOUT 2 DOZEN • TIME: 4 HOURS

I think we can all agree that the best thing about camping is eating s'mores, right? You can't have a campfire without making s'mores, and in case you didn't know, we have a campfire every night at Camp Half-Blood. What's not to love about s'mores? The crispy honey-cinnamon graham crackers, the gooey, toasted marshmallow, and the creamy melted chocolate: they're messy and tasty and I just can't get enough of them. Now, you might be thinking, WHOA, GROVER, ARE YOU REALLY TRYING TO TEACH US HOW TO MAKE S'MORES? No, no, no. We're gonna make some FANCY s'mores using homemade marshmallows and graham crackers. It may seem like a lot of fuss, but I promise it's easier than it sounds. Plus, you can customize the marshmallows with different flavorings to make your own unique pairings. In this recipe, we use honey to give the marshmallows a rich flavor, but you can swap in corn syrup for that classic, more neutral marshmallow flavor, or you might want to use maple syrup. Try different extracts, too, like mint or orange blossom water—just add ½ to 1 teaspoon in addition to the vanilla extract.

MARSHMALLOWS:
1 cup water, divided
3 tablespoons gelatin powder
1½ cups granulated sugar
1 cup honey
½ teaspoon kosher salt
1 tablespoon vanilla extract
¼ cup powdered sugar, divided
¼ cup cornstarch

GRAHAM CRACKERS:
¾ cup whole wheat flour
¾ cup all-purpose flour
¾ cup dark brown sugar
1 teaspoon kosher salt
½ teaspoon baking soda
¼ teaspoon baking powder
½ teaspoon ground cinnamon

½ cup cold unsalted butter, cubed
¼ cup honey
1 large egg white

Milk chocolate and dark chocolate bars

1. **TO MAKE THE MARSHMALLOWS:** Pour ½ cup of the water into the bowl of a stand mixer fitted with the whisk attachment. Sprinkle the gelatin over the water and let sit for 10 minutes.

2. In a medium saucepan, combine the remaining ½ cup water with the granulated sugar, honey, and salt. Bring the mixture to a boil over medium-high heat, stirring until the sugar is dissolved. Continue boiling, stirring occasionally, about 10 minutes longer, until the honey syrup reaches 240°F.

   The temperature is the important part here—remove from heat once it hits 240°F, whether this happens before or after the 10-minute mark. —Annabeth

3. Turn the mixer full of water and gelatin on to medium-low speed. With the mixer running, slowly stream in the hot honey syrup. Once you've poured in all the syrup, increase the mixer speed to high and beat until the mixture is thick, opaque white, and fluffy, 10 to 15 minutes. Add the vanilla extract and continue mixing until fully incorporated, about 1 minute longer.

4. Lightly grease an 8-by-8-inch baking dish. Scrape the marshmallow mixture into the dish and smooth the top as best you can with a rubber spatula. Dust the top with 2 tablespoons of the powdered sugar. Let the marshmallows sit at room temperature until they are completely set, at least 2 hours and up to 24.

5. In a large bowl, whisk together the remaining powdered sugar and the cornstarch. Transfer the marshmallow slab to a cutting board. Dip a sharp knife in the powdered sugar mixture and cut the marshmallows into squares. Dust the knife with more of the mixture as needed. Toss the cut marshmallows in the powdered sugar mixture to coat. Store homemade marshmallows in an airtight container at room temperature for up to 1 week.

6. **TO MAKE THE GRAHAM CRACKERS:** Preheat the oven to 350°F. Line a half-sheet pan with parchment paper.

7. Combine the whole wheat and all-purpose flours with the ¾ cup brown sugar, salt, baking soda, baking powder, cinnamon, and butter in the bowl of a food processor. Pulse until the mixture resembles wet sand, 2 to 3 minutes. Add the honey and the egg white and pulse until a smooth dough forms, 2 to 3 minutes longer.

8. Place a sheet of parchment paper on a clean work surface. Tip the dough out onto the parchment and pat it into a rough rectangle shape. Lay a second sheet of parchment on top and roll the dough out to a thickness of about ⅛ inch. Transfer the dough, parchment and all, to a half-sheet pan. Chill it in the freezer for 10 to 15 minutes, until firm.

9. Use a square cookie cutter to stamp out 2-by-2-inch squares from the dough. Transfer the squares to the prepared pan, leaving about ½ inch between them. Continue gathering up the scraps, rolling them out, chilling the rolled-out dough, and cutting out squares until you have enough to fill the pan.

10. Perforate the graham cracker squares with a fork, piercing them all the way through. Bake the graham crackers until they are golden and set, 15 to 18 minutes. Let the crackers cool in the pan for 5 minutes, then transfer them to a wire cooling rack to cool completely. Repeat this process until you've used up all the dough. Store the crackers in an airtight container at room temperature for up to 1 week.

11. **TO MAKE S'MORES:** Heat the oven to 400°F and line a half-sheet pan with parchment paper. Put down as many graham crackers as you like, and top half of them with squares of milk or dark chocolate—leave the other half of the crackers bare so they get warm and slightly toasted. Top the chocolate with a marshmallow and bake until the marshmallow is puffed and golden, 2 to 4 minutes.

12. Place a graham cracker on top of each toasted marshmallow to create a sandwich. Let the s'mores cool slightly before eating them.

EGG CREAM

YIELD: 1 DRINK ▪ TIME: 3 MINUTES ▪ V, GF

This sweet drink isn't quite as creamy or dense as chocolate milk. It's light, frothy, and still plenty chocolaty. The foam created by stirring together the milk and fizzy water kinda reminds me of sea foam, which might explain why a certain son of Poseidon likes them so much.

Contrary to the name, there is no egg or cream in this egg cream. I suppose one or both ingredients may have been included back when the drink was invented by Eastern European Jewish immigrants in New York City in the late 1800s. The more common variety still found today is made of just three ingredients: flavored syrup, milk, and seltzer or club soda. I'm not sure why mortals haven't changed the name in all this time. But I do know a great recipe for one.

2 to 3 tablespoons chocolate syrup	½ cup cold milk (any %)	1 cup ice-cold seltzer or club soda

1. In a tall glass, stir the chocolate syrup and the milk together until they are fully combined.

2. While stirring constantly, slowly add the seltzer or club soda. Serve immediately.

FLORAL LOTUS COOKIES

YIELD: ABOUT 2 DOZEN · TIME: 1 HOUR 15 MINUTES · V

Lotus Eaters get their name from the actual lotus flowers and fruits that they eat, which make them forget all their troubles and live in blissfully ignorant apathy. Live your Lotus Eater fantasy, though not quite as extreme, with these lotus-like treats. For these little flower-shaped cookies, we use a base flavor of raspberry, which pairs really nicely with floral flavors like rose and orange blossom. Those flavors, in turn, pair nicely with pistachio. Mix them all together, and you get a cookie that's fruity, nutty, with little hints of floral and citrus notes that, with just one bite, will make all your cares just drift away. By the time you finish that cookie, you'll be feeling a little better, calmer—like you just finished a heroic quest, or finished cooking your way through an entire cookbook. We promise these won't make you forget your life in the outside world. No, really. C'mon, just one bite.

½ cup raw pistachios

1 cup unsalted butter, room temperature

¾ cup granulated sugar

¾ teaspoon kosher salt

2 large egg whites, room temperature

1 teaspoon vanilla extract

½ teaspoon orange blossom water

½ teaspoon rose water

2 cups all-purpose flour

¼ cup freeze-dried raspberry powder

1. Heat the oven to 350°F. Spread the pistachios out on a half-sheet pan and bake them until they are lightly toasted and fragrant, about 10 minutes. Let the nuts cool, then finely grind them in a food processor or chop them finely with a knife. Set the pistachio powder aside.

2. In a large bowl, using a handheld electric mixer set on high speed, cream together the butter, sugar, and salt until the mixture is light and creamy, 3 to 5 minutes. Add the egg whites and beat until the mixture is smooth, about 2 more minutes. Then, beat in the vanilla extract, orange blossom water, and rose water.

3. Reduce the mixer speed to low and add in the flour, the freeze-dried raspberry powder, and the reserved finely ground pistachio powder until a soft, smooth dough forms and no streaks of dry flour remain. Be careful not to overmix.

4. Lay a sheet of parchment paper on a clean work surface. Tip the dough onto the parchment and shape and pat it into a rough rectangle shape. Lay another sheet of parchment on top and roll out the dough to a thickness of about ¼ inch. Transfer the dough, parchment and all, to the half-sheet pan you used earlier. Chill the dough in the freezer until it is firm, about 10 minutes.

5. Line the half-sheet pan with a fresh sheet of parchment. Take the dough out of the freezer and use a fluted 2-inch round cookie cutter to stamp out as many cookies as you can. Transfer the cookies to the prepared pan, leaving about 1 inch of space between them. Place the cookies back in the freezer to chill for 10 minutes longer.

6. Bake the cookies for 15 to 20 minutes, until they are just turning golden at the edges.

7. Cool the cookies in the pan for 10 minutes, then transfer them to a wire cooling rack to cool completely. Repeat the shaping and baking process with any remaining dough.

These cookies can be stored at room temperature in an airtight container for up to 5 days. —Annabeth

GOOEY BUTTER CAKE

YIELD: ABOUT 12 TO 15 SERVINGS • TIME: 4 HOURS • V

This is a St. Louis specialty that Percy, Annabeth, and I came across as we quested our way through the city. There's something about this delicious ooey-gooey cake; it can take the edge off almost any tense situation, even a Chimera encounter. Again, ALMOST. We decided to learn how to make it and discovered that the original cake may have been created by accident. The story goes that a chef was trying to make a regular cake and accidentally switched the amounts of butter and flour, resulting in something a bit like a brownie, in terms of consistency, but with a buttery, custard-like topping. There are other versions of this special little cake's origin; it's become a bit of a St. Louis myth. The cake is pretty easy to find in restaurants throughout the city—you can even get prepackaged versions in grocery and convenience stores! If you're not in St. Louis, we've got you covered with this recipe. Traditional versions use corn syrup in the filling, but we opted for honey for an extra-flavorful cake.

BASE:
¼ cup warm milk

¼ cup granulated sugar, plus 1 pinch extra

2 teaspoons active dry yeast

1½ teaspoons kosher salt

½ cup butter, softened, plus more for pan

2 large eggs

2 cups all-purpose flour, divided

FILLING:
1 cup butter, softened

1¼ cups granulated sugar

⅓ cup honey

¾ teaspoon kosher salt

2 large eggs, room temperature

1 tablespoon vanilla extract

1¼ cups cake flour, sifted

Powdered sugar, for dusting

1. **TO MAKE THE BASE:** In a small bowl, stir together the warm milk and a pinch of the granulated sugar until the sugar dissolves. Stir in the yeast and let sit for 5 to 10 minutes, until foamy.

2. In the bowl of a stand mixer fitted with a paddle attachment, mix together the ¼ cup granulated sugar with the salt and butter on medium speed until the mixture is smooth and creamy, 2 to 4 minutes. Beat in the eggs, one at a time, until they are incorporated.

3. Reduce the mixer speed to low, then add 1 cup of the all-purpose flour and mix until no dry flour remains. Pour in the milk-and-yeast mixture and beat until smooth. Then add the remaining 1 cup of all-purpose flour, mixing until the dough is smooth and elastic, 5 to 8 minutes.

4. Lightly grease a 9-by-13-inch baking dish with softened unsalted butter.

5. Scrape down the mixer paddle and the sides and bottom of the bowl with a rubber spatula. Fold the batter mixture a few times to make sure the ingredients are well mixed. Then scrape the batter into the baking dish, spreading it to the edges of the pan in an even layer. Cover the pan with plastic wrap and let the base sit at room temperature until it has roughly doubled in volume, about 2 hours. Toward the end of this 2-hour rise time, heat the oven to 350°F and make the filling.

6. **TO MAKE THE FILLING:** In the bowl of a stand mixer fitted with a paddle attachment, combine together the butter, granulated sugar, honey, and salt until the mixture is light and fluffy, 7 to 10 minutes. Beat the eggs in, one at a time, until incorporated, about 1 minute each. Beat in the vanilla extract.

7. Reduce the mixer speed to low and slowly add in the cake flour until it is fully incorporated. Scrape down the paddle and sides and bottom of the bowl with a rubber spatula, then fold the mixture a few times to ensure the ingredients of your filling are all fully incorporated.

8. Use a large spoon to gently dollop this filling over the top of the risen dough base. Gently spread the filling into an even layer. Bake for 25 to 30 minutes, until golden and the center is not quite set—it should gently wobble when you shake the pan.

9. Let the cake cool for 15 to 20 minutes before dusting it with powdered sugar and serving it warm.

SUNFLOWER-BUTTER ROSES

YIELD: 1 DOZEN ▪ TIME: 4 HOURS ▪ V

While Annabeth might appreciate the beauty of a rose, I think she may prefer these edible, flower-inspired treats for their practicality—they're an ideal combination of form and function. With their romantic tone, they could be served at one of the food carts near the Thrill Ride O' Love in Waterland . . . when the park is open, anyway. The dough is similar to the kind used to make babka, another New York City staple, but the filling is made with sweetened sunflower butter, with sunflower seeds for texture, and an exciting burst of chocolate. The sunflower butter is our nod to Apollo and the kids in Cabin 7. (Hey, it never hurts to make allies before the next game of Capture the Flag.) If you'd prefer something different, just swap out the sunflower butter with an equal amount of your favorite nut butter and replace the sunflower seeds with finely chopped roasted nuts.

DOUGH:

4 cups all-purpose flour

1 teaspoon kosher salt

1¼ cups lukewarm milk

2 tablespoons honey

2 teaspoons instant yeast

2 large eggs, room temperature

6 tablespoons unsalted butter, softened

FILLING:

¾ cup sunflower butter

¼ cup powdered sugar

Dough (ingredients above)

Filling (ingredients above)

¼ cup shelled, roasted sunflower seeds

½ cup milk chocolate or semi-sweet chocolate, finely chopped

1 large egg white

1 tablespoon water

1. **TO MAKE THE DOUGH:** In the bowl of a stand mixer fitted with the dough hook attachment, whisk together the flour and salt.

2. In a separate small bowl, combine the milk and honey and stir to mix them well, then stir in the yeast until it dissolves.

3. With the mixer running on low speed, pour the yeast mixture into the flour mixture, and then add the eggs.

4. Mix until a shaggy dough forms, then increase the speed to medium. Knead until the dough is soft and smooth, 5 to 7 minutes. Then, with the mixer still running, add the unsalted butter, 2 tablespoons at a time, allowing each portion of the butter to become fully incorporated before adding the next. Continue mixing on medium speed until the dough is smooth, elastic, and glossy, 10 to 15 minutes longer.

5. Transfer the dough to a greased bowl and cover it. Let the dough sit at room temperature until it has doubled in volume, 60 to 90 minutes.

6. Grease a standard, 12-cup muffin or cupcake tin.

7. **TO MAKE THE FILLING:** In a medium bowl, combine the sunflower butter and the powdered sugar and beat until smooth and creamy. Set aside.

8. **TO MAKE THE SUNFLOWER-BUTTER ROSES:** Tip the dough out onto a lightly floured work surface and roll it out to a 12-by-24-inch rectangle. Spread the sunflower-butter filling over the surface of the dough.

9. Sprinkle the sunflower seeds and chocolate over the top of the filling.

10. Fold the dough in half to make a 12-by-12-inch square. Using a bench scraper or pizza cutter, start at the folded edge and cut the dough into twelve 1-inch wide sections.

11. Grab one strip of filled dough by its ends and gently twist a few times to create a spiral. Coil the spiral into one of the cups of the muffin tin, tucking the ends into the bottom. Repeat with the remaining strips of dough.

12. Drape the pan with a lightly greased sheet of plastic wrap and let the rolls rise until they are well-puffed, but not quite doubled in volume, about 1 hour.

13. Beat the egg white and water together in a small bowl. Brush the tops of the rolls with the egg wash, then bake until they are golden, 18 to 22 minutes. If you're unsure whether the rolls are done, insert an instant-read thermometer into the center of one of the rolls—it should register 190°F. Let them cool for 10 minutes in the pan before transferring the rolls to a wire cooling rack to cool completely.

RIZOGALO

YIELD: 4 TO 6 SERVINGS ▪ TIME: 1 HOUR ▪ V, GF

This recipe comes courtesy of the campers in Cabin 4. I'd describe it as a particularly inviting Greek version of rice pudding. Rizogalo translates to "rice milk"—an appropriate name, since those are the first two ingredients. Making this is fun, since all you really have to do is overcook rice in too much milk. It sounds like the kind of recipe that was invented by accident, but I've come to trust that the children of Demeter don't make mistakes when it comes to grains. Anyway, the resulting pudding is thick, creamy, and full of extra-tender grains of rice. This recipe includes warm, aromatic cinnamon, fragrant vanilla, and honey for sweetness.

This pudding is great either warm or cold, but it does take a few hours to chill, so be sure to plan ahead if you want to serve it cold. —Annabeth

---

1 cup arborio rice
4½ cups milk

1 cup heavy cream
or half-and-half
1 cinnamon stick

1 vanilla bean pod
¾ cup honey
¼ teaspoon kosher salt

---

1. In a medium saucepan, stir together the rice, milk, cream, and cinnamon stick.

2. Cut the vanilla bean in half lengthwise. Use the back of a knife to scrape out the vanilla seeds. Add the seeds and pod to the saucepan.

3. Bring the milk and rice to a simmer over medium heat, then reduce heat to maintain a gentle simmer. Cover the pan and let the mixture cook, stirring occasionally, until the rice is tender, 20 to 25 minutes.

4. Stir in the honey and salt. Continue cooking, stirring occasionally, until the pudding has thickened and the rice is very soft, but still has a slight chew, 15 to 20 minutes longer. Let the rizogalo cool slightly before serving it warm, or transfer it to an airtight container and refrigerate it for at least 4 hours to serve cold.

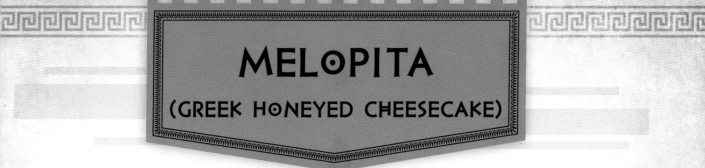

MELOPITA
(GREEK HONEYED CHEESECAKE)

YIELD: 8 TO 12 SERVINGS ▪ TIME: 1 HOUR 30 MINUTES ▪ V, GF

The starring role of any cheesecake usually goes to, understandably, the cheese. In melopita, a traditional Greek cheesecake, honey is the co-star. Since honey is so heavily favored by the gods, this is the kind of recipe an aspiring hero might want to keep in their back pocket. While cream cheese is what's most commonly used in many cheesecakes, this version is traditionally made with a fresh Greek cheese, like mizithra or anthotyros. Those can be a bit tricky to find, but you can use ricotta as a good substitute if your search for Greek cheese comes up empty. This cheesecake is crustless, which saves some steps, and it's really easy to whip up with just a mixing bowl and spoon or whisk—no electric mixer required!

1½ pounds mizithra or ricotta cheese, room temperature

4 large eggs, room temperature

⅓ cup honey, plus more for serving

1 teaspoon orange zest

1½ tablespoons cornstarch

½ teaspoon ground cinnamon, plus more for serving

¼ teaspoon kosher salt

1 tablespoon orange juice

2 teaspoons vanilla extract

½ teaspoon orange blossom water

1. Preheat the oven to 325°F. Lightly grease an 8-inch springform pan, and line the bottom with an 8-inch round of parchment paper.

2. In a large mixing bowl, stir together the cheese, eggs, honey, and orange zest until smooth.

3. In a small bowl, whisk together the cornstarch, cinnamon, and salt, breaking apart any clumps. Whisk in the orange juice, vanilla extract, and orange blossom water until smooth.

4. Pour the orange juice mixture from your small bowl into your large bowl containing the cheese mixture. Stir until all ingredients are incorporated.

5. Scrape the resulting batter into the prepared pan, smoothing the top with the back of a spoon or spatula. Bake until golden and set, with just a slight wobble in the very center of the cheesecake, 50 to 60 minutes.

6. Let the cheesecake cool for about 15 minutes, then run a knife around the edge to separate it from the pan. Release the sides of the pan from the base.

7. Drizzle the cheesecake with honey, sprinkle it with cinnamon, and serve it warm or at room temperature.

EPILOGUE

You've done it, heroes! You made it to the end of the book, and congratulations are in order. Whether you created every single dish in the book (whoa, HUGE congrats if you did that!) or just tried your hand at something new, learned a skill, or found a new favorite meal, you should be proud of your accomplishments!

As for me, Percy, and Annabeth, we had quite a time gathering all these recipes. We laughed, we cried, we grew as people (or satyr, in my case), and things were pretty touch and go for a while there. Honestly, things were pretty touch and go for almost the entire quest.

It's a relief to be back safe and sound at Camp Half-Blood. And it's even better to get to enjoy the dryads' cooking again. Percy, Annabeth, and I have always appreciated the hard work they put into our meals. But after having to fend for ourselves while literally fighting for our lives at every turn . . . it's really taken our appreciation to a new level. And that extends to really anybody willing to cook for us. Now that we've got all these slick skills in the kitchen, hopefully we can repay the favor.

But first, rest. So much rest. I wanna sleep for a week!

GLOSSARY

GLOSSARY OF TERMS, TOOLS, INGREDIENTS, AND TECHNIQUES

ACTIVE DRY YEAST: Available in ¼-ounce packages that contain 2¼ teaspoons yeast. Always check the date on the package to make sure the yeast is truly active.

CAKE FLOUR: Milled from soft wheat and containing cornstarch, cake flour is low in protein and high in starch. It gives cakes a light crumb. Cake flour has also undergone a bleaching process that increases its ability to hold water and sugar, so cakes made with cake flour are less likely to fall.

DOUGH HOOK: Some mixers have a dough hook that moves in an attached bowl; others have a bowl that revolves on a small platter. The size of the bowl is important. If you are going to bake large amounts, carefully check the details of your mixer.

DUTCH OVEN: A large, heavy cooking pot usually made of cast iron. This can go on the stove or in the oven and is great at retaining heat.

FOOD PROCESSOR: An electric kitchen tool that consists of a plastic bowl fitted over a set of spinning blades, which can be used to assist in a variety of food prep, including chopping, shredding, pulverizing, mixing, and more. It's commonly (but not exclusively) used to prep dry ingredients before cooking.

FRY STATION AND SAFETY: If you're making something that requires deep frying, here are some important tips to prevent you from setting your house (and yourself) on fire:

- If you don't have a dedicated deep fryer, use a Dutch oven or a high-walled sauté pan.
- Never have too much oil in the pan! You don't want hot oil spilling out as soon as you put the food in.
- Use only a suitable cooking oil, like canola, peanut, or vegetable oil.
- Always keep track of the oil temperature with a thermometer. 350°F to 375°F should do the trick.
- Never put too much food in the pan at the same time!
- Never put wet food or utensils in the pan. Hot oil will splatter as a result and may cause burns.
- Always have a lid nearby to cover the pan in case it starts to spill over or catch fire. A properly rated fire extinguisher is also great to have on hand in case of emergencies.
- Never leave the pan unattended and never let children near the pan.
- Never, ever put your face, hand, or any other body part in the hot oil.

INSTANT YEAST: A second kind of active dry yeast, called INSTANT YEAST, is three times more powerful than active dry yeast. Also called EUROPEAN YEAST, it is a stronger, more stable yeast developed for commercial bakers. Some bakers feel that it should not be used in sweet bread doughs or those that require long, slow risings.

KNEAD: Uncover the dough and knead it by using the heel of one hand to push the dough away from you and then pulling the dough back toward you with your fingertips. Turn the dough and repeat these steps until it is smooth and elastic.

MARINATE: This refers to the process of soaking food, often meat or vegetables, in a seasoned liquid before you plan to cook it. Often, the marinade will contain something acidic like vinegar, which can give your food additional flavor and help tenderize meat.

MIXER: Two basic types of motor-driven electric mixers are available, stand mixers and handheld (or portable) mixers. Each has its place in the kitchen. Stand mixers are stationary machines good for large amounts and heavy batters.

REDUCE: Simmering or boiling a liquid, such as broth, is a good way to enhance flavor. As liquid simmers, its quantity decreases, and the liquid thickens into a flavorful sauce.

RISE: Often, but not always, bread dough rises two times. Some breads have a very long first rise followed by a shorter rising after shaping. Other times, breads rest for only a short while before shaping and then rise much longer in the second stage. The important thing is that the dough is well-risen when it's time to bake it. You can always slow down the rising by keeping the dough cool. Another aspect of rising to keep in mind is that a firm dough usually rises more slowly than a moist dough.

SAUTÉ: Taken from the French verb meaning "to jump," this is the process of cooking quickly in a small amount of fat. Your pan should be preheated with the fat before adding foods so that they sear quickly. There should be plenty of room in the pan so that the food doesn't get crowded and can simmer in its own juices.

SHIMMERING: This describes heated cooking oil that gleams and moves in ripples. It may indicate that the oil has reached an approximate temperature of 275°F.

ZEST: Can be both a noun and a verb. ZEST is the name of the colorful peel of citrus fruits that is used as a seasoning; it's also the name of the process of scraping a microplane grater across citrus fruit in order to shred its peel.

ABOUT THE AUTHOR

Jarrett Melendez grew up on the mean, deer-infested streets of Bucksport, Maine. A former chef and line cook, Jarrett has worked in restaurants, diners, and bakeries throughout New England and Mexico, and got instruction on Japanese home cooking from some very patient host mothers when he lived in Tokyo and Hiroshima. He's been a professional writer since 2009, but started working as a recipe developer and food writer in 2020. His work has appeared on *Bon Appétit*, *Saveur*, Epicurious, and Food52, and he is the author of *My Pokémon Baking Book* and *RuneScape: The Official Cookbook*.

When not cooking and writing about food, Jarrett is also an award-winning comic book writer. His best-known work is *Chef's Kiss* from Oni Press, which won the Alex Award from the American Library Association and a GLAAD award nomination for Outstanding Graphic Novel, in addition to being nominated for an Eisner Award for Best Publication for Teens. Jarrett has contributed to the Ringo-nominated *All We Ever Wanted*, *Full Bleed*, *Young Men in Love*, and *Murder Hobo: Chaotic Neutral*. He is currently working on *Tales of the Fungo: The Legend of Cep*, a middle-grade fantasy adventure, to be published by Andrews McMeel.

He lives in Massachusetts with his collection of Monokuro Boo plush pigs.

ACKNOWLEDGMENTS

To all of the found family that have helped me along on my own quest, but especially Sara, whose knowledge of Greek food saved the day more than once. Thanks for being the Wise Girl to my Seaweed Brain.

DIETARY CONSIDERATIONS

V = VEGETARIAN • V+ = VEGAN • GF = GLUTEN-FREE
* = IF FOLLOWING MODIFIED INSTRUCTIONS

MEASUREMENT CONVERSIONS

VOLUME

US	METRIC
⅓ teaspoon (tsp)	1 mL
1 teaspoon (tsp)	5 mL
1 tablespoon (tbsp)	15 mL
1 fluid ounce (fl. oz.)	30 mL
⅕ cup	50 mL
¼ cup	60 mL
⅔ cup	80 mL
3.4 fluid ounces (fl. oz.)	100 mL
½ cup	120 mL
⅓ cup	160 mL
¾ cup	180 mL
1 cup	240 mL
1 pint (2 cups)	480 mL
1 quart (4 cups)	.95 liter

WEIGHT

OUNCES	GRAMS
.5 ounce (oz.)	14 grams (g)
1 ounce (oz.)	28 grams (g)
¼ pound (lb.)	113 grams (g)
⅓ pound (lb.)	151 grams (g)
½ pound (lb.)	227 grams (g)
1 pound (lb.)	454 grams (g)

TEMPERATURES

FAHRENHEIT	CELSIUS
200°F	93°C
212°F	100°C
250°F	121°C
275°F	135°C
300°F	149°C
325°F	163°C
350°F	177°C
400°F	204°C
425°F	218°C
450°F	232°C
475°F	246°C

INSIGHT
EDITIONS

PO Box 3088
San Rafael, CA 94912
www.insighteditions.com

 Find us on Facebook: www.facebook.com/InsightEditions
 Follow us on Instagram: @insighteditions

ISBN: 979-8-88663-608-6

Publisher: Raoul Goff
SVP, Group Publisher: Vanessa Lopez
VP, Creative: Chrissy Kwasnik
VP, Manufacturing: Alix Nicholaeff
Designer: Brooke McCullum
Editor: Alexis Sattler
Editorial Assistant: Jennifer Pellman
VP, Senior Executive Project Editor: Vicki Jaeger
Production Manager: Deena Hashem
Senior Production Manager, Subsidiary Rights: Lina s Palma-Temena

Photography by Waterbury Publications, Inc.

ROOTS of PEACE   REPLANTED PAPER

Insight Editions, in association with Roots of Peace, will plant two trees for each tree used in the manufacturing of this book. Roots of Peace is an internationally renowned humanitarian organization dedicated to eradicating land mines worldwide and converting war-torn lands into productive farms and wildlife habitats. Roots of Peace will plant two million fruit and nut trees in Afghanistan and provide farmers there with the skills and support necessary for sustainable land use.

Manufactured in China by Insight Editions

10 9 8 7 6 5 4 3 2